Till Death Do Us Part or Something Else Comes Up

Till Death Do Us Part
or Something Else
Comes Up

by
ZANE ALEXANDER

THE WESTMINSTER PRESS
PHILADELPHIA

BOOK DESIGN BY DOROTHY E. JONES

PUBLISHED BY THE WESTMINSTER PRESS®
PHILADELPHIA, PENNSYLVANIA

PRINTED IN THE UNITED STATES OF AMERICA

Library of Congress Cataloging in Publication Data

Alexander, Zane, 1934–
    Till death do us part or something else comes up.

    1. Marriage—United States I. Title.
HQ536.A53   301.42'0973   76–16851
ISBN 0–664–24750–4

To Gloria and Donna and Dawn

CONTENTS

Introduction

Even to the casual observer, it is apparent that something is wrong with many marriages in the United States. The divorce rate is accelerating. In 1867 there were 10,000 divorces. In 1948 there were 421,000. In that time-frame the population increased 300 percent, marriages increased 400 percent, and the divorce rate increased 4,000 percent. Today the divorce rate is approaching 40 percent. As you move from east to west, the divorce rate increases. The same is true from north to south. (*Journal of Marriage and the Family,* May 1971, p. 321.) By the time you reach Southern California, the southwestern tip of our country, divorce occurs at a ratio of 10 to 12.

In 1971, 2,000 Americans killed their spouses. This was 12 percent of all murders committed that year. ("Family Fighting," in *Marriage and Family Living,* April 1974.) In 1973, more police were killed investigating family quarrels than any other type of police activity. (National Institute of Law Enforcement and Criminal Justice.) The second leading cause of police fatalities was pursuing armed robbers. So in 1973, it was safer to pursue an armed bank robber than it was to intervene in a family quarrel.

My clinical experience in marriage and family counseling

over the past fourteen years also leads me to the conclusion that something is basically wrong. The purpose of this book is to analyze the structure of the institution of marriage and to make recommendations to improve the quality of married life.

I propose to do this by telling case stories—a unique literary format that offers the writer an excellent structure for communicating data of survival significance. In case stories the writer unites elements of many actual case studies until a theme emerges that he can develop into a fictional format. Case stories can communicate a broader theme than is possible with the simple narration of a single case study. If the case story is well written, a hundred different people will say, "Hey, that's me!" The case story also allows the writer to weave into the plot autobiographical material, so the writer is able to draw on both his clinical experience and his own life.

It is my intention that these stories will enable the reader to gain insights from my experience and from my life that will help to focus more sharply the fuzzy image of the institution of marriage. I intend for the stories to be a mirror of the condition of married life in the United States. Comments and questions are added at the end of each story both to serve as discussion starters for groups that use this book as an outline for their interactions and also to guide the reader in his reflections upon some possible implications of the stories. The comments and questions are not meant to summarize the meaning of the case story but rather to initiate thought patterns that will be relevant to human life.

Part 5, "What to Do About It," contains practical recommendations that will help to improve married life and, it is hoped, will enable the most important institution of our culture to survive.

1
Husbands Don't Last Forever

Thε PεrFεct WiFε

Jane had known for a year that John was going to die. Death had systematically invaded every inch of his heart chamber. The final surrender was only a matter of time. She knew all this in her head but she refused to believe it in her bones. John had burned his way through life and Jane assumed that the fire could not go out. She knew that this assumption had no reality but she lived as if it did.

John was a hardworking stockbroker who lived in Lake Forest, Illinois. He was the eighth of ten children and had learned very early that he must blast his way into relationships. The "must" was not so, but John consistently told himself that it was. He learned that he could get attention through bombast and at the same time keep people from getting too close. Although he wanted people around, he insisted upon controlling the interactions. He was warmhearted and generous but there was little flow to his life-style. John was bumpy. He wanted to make contact but he refused to let people come inside. Although he could initiate contact with people, he couldn't hold it. He bounced from person to person.

Jane had never seen John cry. One night while he was sitting at the kitchen table his body began to shake. Volcanic

13

heaves shook his chest. He overlapped his arms and tried to squeeze back the eruption.

"John, why don't you let it out?" Jane pleaded. He did. John confessed his deepest fears. There was little money. Jane wasn't old enough to draw social security. His pension was small. He had been overprotective of Jane all these years and now he was dying. Their meager financial resources had been exhausted on his medical bills. They were deeply in debt. Their credit was gone. Soon he would be gone too.

Six months later John died from his fifth heart attack. In the meantime, Jane had done nothing. She had no marketable skills and only a meager income. There were no children, so Jane found herself deprived of her only support.

At the funeral home Jane continued to avoid the reality that John was dead. She was overly particular about the way his tie fitted. She talked about the pretty casket and the lovely flowers. She consistently failed to face the hard, cold fact that John was dead. All of her adult years she had leaned upon one prop and now she could not bring herself to believe that her sole support was gone.

Jane was everything her culture wanted her to be: faithful wife, loyal friend, kind and thoughtful neighbor, devout Methodist, and a law-abiding Republican. And no one ever saw her leaning upon John as an idolatrous relationship, nor did she. She assumed that her role as obedient and loving wife could have no imperfections. She also assumed that her husband would last forever. Jane knew the Ten Commandments. She had learned both the words and the meaning of them in her confirmation classes. "Thou shalt have no other gods before me." (Ex. 20:3.) This meant that you weren't supposed to worship idols, as the natives did in darkest Africa. But it didn't mean that she wasn't supposed to worship John. Of course she was an adoring wife; she adored John. Her friends said she worshiped the ground he walked on, and she would

14

have quickly agreed. But this wasn't idolatry. Idolatry was something black people did in Africa. Besides, she had given to support foreign missionaries ever since she was a little girl. No one could say she had not done her part to stop idolatry. But worshiping John was different. John was her husband.

Jane leaned upon John and her leaning was a total emotional dependency. John leaned too, so their marriage was an A-frame relationship. John could not express all of this in words, but that night sitting in the kitchen he was flooded with sadness when he realized that his death would destroy half of the A and that Jane would be leaning on nothing more than a memory. He knew then that he had become Jane's god and that when your god dies, your life is ruined.

For the first week after John died, the perfect wife was the perfect widow. She held up remarkably well at the funeral and was a gracious hostess to the numerous people who stopped by after the services. She was more than patient with John's lawyer, who began the process of settling the estate. Apart from their house in Lake Forest and a lot on a lake in Wisconsin, there was little to settle, but Jane had no concern for money. She knew she would have two hundred dollars a month that she could count on and she felt that she could take care of what she really needed with this amount of money. The bills would just have to wait until she could sell the lot in Wisconsin.

Jane knew that she would miss John, but she had no idea how much or in what ways. At first she was too busy with the funeral and the estate to have time to hurt. Then for several weeks the neighbors and relatives flooded her with attention. A month after the funeral her company began to disappear. She could stay busy during the day, but there was little to do at night. The house seemed twice as big as it did before, but there was no way she would part with it. The house was all that she had left. Without it she would not have been able to occupy herself even during the day. The house was both her salvation and her perdition. It was spooky at night and it reminded her of John during the day. It just wasn't fair for John to be snatched away from her so early in life. She began to think of other couples and other husbands who were older than John who were in the best of health. Her anger began to feed upon her loneliness. The more time she had to think, the more her plight seemed unfair. She and John had been such good Methodists. He had never been unfaithful to her or to the church. Why did God take him when she needed him so much? And why were all the dirty old men in Lake Forest still alive and chasing younger women?

When Jane forced herself to get out of the house she was either alone on the streets or shoved about by endless couples. Before John died, she had not noticed this endless milling of couples in stores and shops. When she would wait in line at a check-out counter, there would be a couple in front of her and one behind her and they would be talking to each other but never to her. Jane was a displaced person in coupledom and she wanted to scream, "Hey, I'm still a human being and I have as much right to companionship as anybody." But she never did.

"Oh, excuse me!" the lady behind her said when she bumped Jane with her cart. She had been so busy talking to her husband that she had not noticed Jane.

"That's O.K.," Jane said. It wasn't really O.K. and Jane could not hold back the tears.

"All I did was bump her," the lady complained. "You'd think I had run over her with a truck."

Jane pushed her cart to the side and walked quickly the way embarrassed people do. She didn't feel like eating anyway. She felt like dying. And each day she died a little bit faster. Her loneliness screamed for relief, but no one was listening and Jane was too nice a person to shout for help.

Comments

Jane is hurting for many reasons. She refused to recognize her overdependence on John and she consistently refused to do anything about it. She lived in a romantic dreamworld, and if pressed on this point, she would have admitted it. She lacked awareness that she had been carefully conditioned to live this way. She assumed that her emotional and spiritual dependence on John was an act of her own doing. Jane could have chosen to lean less on John. In no way was she forced by her culture or community into her life-style, but there was a systematic conditioning of her thought patterns. She let herself be romanticized. She let the media and the market-place shape her life-style into a pattern that was not functional for growing old. She became a romanticist.

Institutional romanticism is the structuring of society into dyads with the assumption that two people can meet all of each other's interpersonal needs, and, like institutional racism, it causes pain. The pain is a deep, hollow ache. Much of the pathos is that the people who hurt blame themselves and not the institution. When the oppressed manage to escape masochistic patterns, they frequently blame God, so either their inner selves or their faith patterns take a beating. Jane's faith took the full force of the storm, but her grief work was delayed and her faith became a passive whipping post rather than an active support.

Questions

In what respects is the cultural ideal of the American marriage idolatrous?

What sorts of things do you do to avoid facing unpleasant realities?

What is the source of such notions as: Men never cry. Always be polite. Women should not assert themselves.

What personal needs can be fulfilled in a dyad relationship? What needs cannot be?

What is your concept of a perfect wife?

The Good Girl

Barbara knew the question was coming. She prayed to God that it wouldn't, but it did. Susie was standing on the transmission hump in the back seat. Although Barbara anticipated her question as she stopped at the light, there was no way that she could hold it back.

"Mommy, you still like Daddy a little bit, don't you?"

All of Barbara's guilt feelings about the divorce focused sharp and clear: "Good wives don't divorce their husbands." "Good mothers don't deprive their children of a father." "Good Christians should put their own needs last." She was flooded by a torrent of parental oughts and shoulds. She ought to be a good girl and not cause any trouble.

"Just eat your supper and don't ask so many questions" came back to the foreground of her consciousness.

"Mommy, you do, don't you?" the five-year-old insisted.

"Yes, Susie, I like Daddy a little bit," Barbara said as she shifted into second gear. "Daddy and I have just decided not to live together anymore."

Barbara was twenty-nine, had two years of college and a brand-new divorce. She was an intensely sensitive and responsive woman whose slender frame carried more than her share of parental put-downs and religious restrictions. Her life-style could be summed up in one sentence, "Don't get your dress dirty," and until her divorce she hadn't. Now there was a dark, dirty stain and Barbara had exhausted herself trying to wash it out.

To make things worse, Barbara's ex-husband was a good guy. He was a hardworking electrical engineer who provided well for his family and came home every night like a faithful canine. He also had the aesthetic sensitivity of a bluetick hound dog. His biological organs worked well, but his awareness of Barbara's artistic and emotional repertoire was nil.

Barbara double-clutched as she shifted into third gear, something she didn't do very often.

From the very start their sex life had been little more than a gymnastic exercise in which Joe relieved himself of his semen and then went back to his studies at the dining room table. Sex lasted at most two or three minutes and when Barbara began to lose interest in this nocturnal brevity, Joe branded her as frigid. For five years she accepted the sentence. Like a good girl she ate her supper and didn't ask any questions.

If she had not met an art student from Mexico City, she might have died thinking her sexual dysfunction was all her fault. He was parked behind her one night at the art lab. When her car wouldn't start, he offered her a ride home. The following weekend he asked her to join him at a local exhibit of his drawings. She did. And from that weekend their friendship grew until eventually they made love.

Barbara felt guilty about the double life she was living. For the first six months of the affair she expected the long finger of God publicly to point her out and push her down in an experience of shame and humiliation, but to her surprise, everything went great. Joe was preoccupied with his work and had no awareness of her new relationship at school. Barbara made several halfhearted attempts to end the affair

20

but when nothing catastrophic had happened by the end of the first year, she began to enjoy herself for the first time in her life. Joe would always be there with his slide rule and paycheck. Her other needs for sex and companionship were being met at school.

Barbara shifted to fourth gear and glanced in her rearview mirror to see what Susie was doing.

It had all been so beautiful until Joe was offered a promotion if he would move to Detroit. And then her world went schizoid. "No, I don't want to move at all!" Barbara cried.

"I can't understand you. A five-thousand-dollar raise and you don't want me to take it. What the hell is going on with you?"

It was then that Barbara told him. She had expected to be thrown out of the house, but after the initial explosion, which contained the word "whore," Joe made a remarkable turnaround. He apologized repeatedly for his anger and promised her anything if she would go with him to Detroit. Even as she packed, Barbara knew that the marriage would never work.

They lived in Detroit for three years and Barbara was miserable every moment. She refused to have sex with Joe, and his most sincere efforts to make up for his past indifference only annoyed her more. She slowly grew to despise him. The end of their relationship was inevitable and Barbara desperately wanted the courage to pronounce the benediction and be civil about it. She was much afraid that Joe would not be civil. She was fearful of the storm. Deep inside she feared that Joe would call her a bad girl or, worse still, an unworthy mother.

For some reason Barbara made no preparation at all for that day when she would have to support herself. She had leaned on Joe for so long that leaning had become a life-style. She was miserable with Joe and at the same time terrified of leaving him. Was there anyone she could lean on if she did? Her mental processes never included the concept, "I don't have to lean on anyone." There had always been some significant male in her life who would take care of her. Although she had never found fulfillment in this way of life, she lacked the courage to say, "Enough!" She also lacked the incentive to develop a skill that would financially support her in the marketplace. Leaners don't do well in the American marketplace and Barbara knew it. Mentally and physically she was equipped to compete with anyone. She had everything the marketplace wanted: youth, intelligence, beauty plus a warm and outgoing personality. She was a WASP with two years of college but she had let a chauvinistic culture pull out her stinger. If she had taken a personality test, she would have scored well because tests don't measure courage. She had become a nonperson living a nonlife in a noncommunity.

Barbara began each day saying to herself: "I'm miserable and unhappy but I can't leave Joe. I just can't." And her friends bought into her self-deception. Most of them were living nonlives too. The next-door neighbor, who was sympathetic and supportive, and Barbara spent endless hours talking about how awful their husbands were. They structured their time in a marathon excursion of their mutual misery. At least it was company. Barbara would not share her marriage failure with her parents. Since good girls don't have unsuccessful marriages, she chose not to tarnish this image. With the passage of time she began to hurt more. She learned that time heals nothing. She went to see her minister, a portly old priest who Barbara felt certain would comfort her in a passive pastoral way.

"Barbara, I don't believe a word you're saying," he said, without blinking, halfway through her third visit.

"I don't know what you mean," Barbara lied. She knew

exactly what he meant. He wasn't sucked in by her helplessness.

"Barbara, I believe that you can leave Joe any day you want to. I believe that you are staying with Joe because you are choosing to do so." Then he added, "Barbara, I want you to look at yourself in the mirror every morning this week and say, 'I am living with Joe Simpson because I am choosing to do so.' "

Barbara repeated this litany of reality for two weeks. The third week she got a job and the fourth week she went to see a lawyer. She paused for what seemed like a long time before she opened the door to the lawyer's office. She started to walk away. Somewhere deep inside herself she found some long-dormant courage. Slowly Barbara repeated to herself, "I am choosing to live no longer with Joe Simpson." She twisted the doorknob and felt a rush of fresh air inside herself.

"Mommy, when are we ever going to get to that garage?" Susie interrupted her thoughts. Barbara turned left on Westwood Avenue and at the same time replied, "It won't be long now, dear."

The transition from dependent housewife to divorced secretary had not been easy. Barbara found that she must cultivate not only new friends but a different kind of people. The superstraight suburban housewives of Detroit lived in a different world from the nineteen-year-old secretaries in her office. There was a raw earthiness about the marketplace that she had not been exposed to before. And for a long time she felt above this jungle of human vulgarity. Her newfound peers were sensitive to this superiority and carefully ostracized this envoy from suburbia. At the same time that she felt left out by women, she felt smothered by men. Barbara learned that with chauvinists there is an open season on divorcées. She had been without sex for so long that she found it hard to say no, so she often had sex when her enlightened self-interest might have dictated a stalling tactic.

The Volkswagen behind her was impatiently honking for her to respond to the green light in front of her. Her foot lifted from the clutch while she scowled in her mirror at the man behind her who turned out to be a woman. The garage was only two or three stores down on the right, so Barbara concentrated on her driving and insisted that Susie be quiet for a moment. Barbara waited for the better part of an hour while the orange-suited mechanics replaced her muffler. Someone had told her that the damn thing would kill her if she didn't get it fixed. The orange-suited men had said that it couldn't be fixed and that they would have to replace it. Barbara didn't trust men mechanics, but it was hard to find females in the muffler business, so she grunted some inaudible sound that the man at the desk took for "O.K."

"Mrs. Simpson, that will be fifty-two dollars and seventy-five cents," the man said. Barbara felt not O.K. down to her toenails. She had less than forty dollars in her checking account and less than ten in her purse. She explained this to the man who impatiently stared down at the cash register.

"Mrs. Simpson, I'll hold your check for one week before I cash it," the man said in tones that reminded her of her math teacher. Barbara nervously wrote out the check and tore it from the book. It tore crooked instead of straight along the perforations.

"Mrs. Simpson, you can't do anything right today, can you?" the man said. A two-word four-letter vulgarity came to Barbara's mind, but she suppressed it. She reached down for Susie's hand and walked out.

24

Comments

The tragedy of the good girl is that she is a warm and wonderful person but lacks the courage to say, "Damn the chauvinists, full speed ahead." She is bounced from one coral reef to another. Although she continues to reach out, each contact hurts. She never touches the terra firma of an authentic relationship and she is afraid to strike out for the open seas of true independence. She is adrift in treacherous waters.

Questions

Why did Barbara find marriage unfulfilling?

What options might have improved her marriage short of divorce?

Having decided on divorce, why does she feel guilty?

How could the church better minister to the personal needs of divorced persons?

What could you do to support yourself if the need arose?

The Angry Spouse

Alice sat with a tear-wet tissue in her hand. It had been a long time since she had cried in the presence of a stranger but the counselor seemed warm and accepting, so she cried. She cried hard. Her tears were a river of liquid fear. Her crying communicated one thing, "I am a scared little girl." She was ambivalent about her present and traumatized about her future. She was reluctant to think about it, but her future looked lonely and devoid of a husband who had always been there.

An attractive forty-year-old woman, Alice had taken good care of herself. She wore chic, contemporary clothes and from outward appearances seemed to be a healthy together person who had managed to find fulfillment as a wife. And from her viewpoint she had. She would never have seen a marriage counselor if Jack had been as content as she was. But Jack was in love with another woman. He had taken a business trip to Seattle, Washington, where he had met an interior decorator.

Jack was a slender but somewhat oversexed business executive who had fantasized promiscuous relationships for years but had never actualized any of them. He had never touched a secretary, never slept with a call girl on a trip. He was a

26

shy and unaggressive person who owed his moderate success to a profound understanding of personnel management. He had struggled hard to complete a degree in business administration at TCU and later an MBA at Texas. If Jack had been required to describe life in one word, he would have said, "Struggle." But Jack could not have won the battle had it not been for Alice. She worked endless hours at endless jobs to see Jack through school. Most of her jobs were clerk positions in department stores. When Alice and Jack had met, she was a clerk at Sanger's in Dallas and he was a clerk at A. Harris. Now, Sanger's and Harris were united and Jack and she were separated.

"We worked so hard that we didn't have time to question whether or not we were happy," Alice sobbed to her counselor. She described how they would prepare supper together after a long, hard day and how she would brew the coffee for his nightly study sessions. "If we weren't happy, at least we were content," she added. "Jack didn't make the best grades but he graduated."

Jack's first fifteen years in the marketplace weren't easy either. He lacked the aggressiveness for sales or production, and had he not specialized in personnel management he would not have survived. As it was, he had to struggle even in personnel, but after fifteen years with the company he had gained a relatively secure position.

"It's not fair," Alice protested. "Just when Jack has it made, he wants to dump me and marry that bitch."

"How do you feel about Jack?"

"Now?"

"Yes, how do you feel about Jack right now?"

"I hate his guts. What he's doing to me is awful. It's terrible and I'm not going to let him get away with it," Alice exploded. "The next time he goes to Seattle will be his last. I won't take him back."

27

"You're really angry with him, aren't you?"

"Well, don't I have a right to be? If your wife did this to you, you'd be angry too."

"Do you want him back?"

Alice paused for a moment, went inside herself, then started crying again. She desperately wanted him back. Although she had assumed that Jack would always be there, she was aware that as their struggle for survival was ending, their relationship was dying. This awareness did nothing to change her behavior. "She's just the same old Alice," her friends said. The only real change that took place in Alice was her intense anger when she learned of Jack's affair.

"Are you aware that you're pushing him away?" the counselor inquired. She wasn't. The counselor pointed out how her anger had so warped her decision-making machinery that she was not acting in a rational manner to save her marriage. On the contrary, she was pushing Jack all the way to Washington. Alice wanted to know what she could do.

"First, you must not assume that Jack will always come home like a good little boy," the counselor said. "Jack comes home because he chooses to do so and he can choose to go somewhere else. And if he does go elsewhere, it's not disgraceful. It may be unpleasant and distasteful but it's not the end of the world." Although Alice knew this, her anger would not let her dwell on it for more than a moment.

"What can I do?" she whined.

"The hard, cold reality is that you must compete with an interior decorator in Seattle, Washington."

"I shouldn't have to compete to keep my own husband," Alice protested.

"The more you tell yourself that, the less chance you have of keeping him. The more you focus on shoulds and should nots rather than on what is, the more your anger gets in the way of making intelligent decisions that will help save your marriage. How do you think your competition acts around Jack?"

"Oh, she's as sweet as syrup."

"How do you act around Jack?"

"You mean, now?" Alice inquired. "Well, I let him know how awful it is that he's doing this to me."

"You're pretty bitchy."

"Well, I have a right to be. After all, I'm his wife."

"How do you think you come off when Jack compares you with your competitor?" Alice refused to hear the question. She had placed all her chips upon one bet. If she maintained an attractive appearance, she could keep him. She felt that the world owed Jack to her. She had earned him even if she were fat and sloppy, but by staying slender and attractive she had purchased his eternal soul. Her dues were paid. Jack couldn't do this to her. Jack was her store-bought possession. She had earned him in a dozen different department stores. Jack owed his education to her, and without his education he would still be selling men's underwear.

"Tell me how to stop him from seeing her." Alice insisted.

"Be sweeter, more interesting, more alive, more exciting than your competition." This wasn't what Alice wanted to hear. She wanted some way to hook Jack's guilt and make him ashamed of his behavior. She wanted to learn how to spank her husband and make him be a good boy.

"If I can talk Jack into coming for counseling, will you tell him to stop seeing her?"

"No way."

"Why not?"

"It wouldn't work."

"What will work?"

"Two things. For you to stop blaming Jack for your anger and for you to change your behavior. You are angry because you are choosing to be angry and you are bitchy toward Jack because you are choosing to be bitchy."

"It isn't fair to the children either." Alice changed the subject. "John especially needs his father. But Jack hardly ever talks to him. He just ignores the kid. Tell me, is that right?"

"Are you angry with me?" the counselor asked.

"No, I'm not angry with you. But you just don't understand. You don't know what it's like to be thrown away."

"Alice, you're right about that. I don't know what a woman feels like when she's thrown away. Would you like to tell me?"

She began to cry again. She made repeated trips to the tissue box on the table in front of her. Rather than take out several at one time, she would remove only one. Quickly it would be wet and unusable. She would then repeat her bend-and-stretch maneuver to get another. In some way this ritual of extracting a solitary tissue made the pain of her hurt a little more bearable.

"What are the tears saying?"

"I don't know what you mean."

"Just let your tears talk," the counselor explained. "If they could talk, what would they say?"

"They'd say, 'I'm losing Jack.' "

"Let them say it."

Alice was hesitant but eventually began to put together some words for her tears. "I am losing Jack and I am scared. I can't stop flowing and I feel that I am being wasted. I wet the tissue and it falls apart. I make everything fall apart."

"What would the tissue say?"

"I'm all wet and soggy. No one wants me after I'm used. Everyone's embarrassed about me. I'm going to be thrown away. I feel all used up. I'm all wrinkled and can't stretch out. People want me only when I'm nice and flat and clean. People don't want me after they have used me."

30

"Does the tissue think it's awful?" the counselor asked.

"Yes, the tissue thinks it's awful." Alice paused. "No, not really, that's just the way it is," she added.

"Let the tissue say that."

"I am all wet and used up and I am going to be thrown away. I don't want to be thrown away but that's just the way it is." Alice cried softly for several minutes and waves of bitterness began to wash out of her. She sat back in the chair and took a deep breath.

"How do you feel?"

"I hurt less. I've got more room inside me. And if Jack leaves, he leaves. That's all there is to it."

"Can you tell me about this extra room you feel inside yourself?"

"There's more air inside me. I can feel my breathing." Alice was introspective for a moment. "My breathing feels good."

Then, sensing that the hour was up and that her marriage was over, Alice found that she could accept both. The end of her marriage was most unpleasant, but if it ended, it ended. She had enjoyed the spadework and regretted that the flower which had bloomed was withering; but flowers do that sometimes even for the best of gardeners.

Comments

Alice had basically one problem: she refused to accept the results of the Civil War. She was a slaveholder! Jack accepted his bondage until he found job security. Then, when the game called survival was over, he exercised his autonomy. A marriage counselor sees this kind of case every day and, although it is his bread and butter, there is a deep sadness that comes

31

from witnessing this aspect of the real world on a daily basis. Even when the rejected spouse is able to pull herself together, as Alice did, a lingering shade of sorrow clouds the counseling room. It is no fun to be thrown away.

Questions

Why do you think Alice was unable to act in a rational manner to save her marriage?

Why is anger a serious problem?

How does suppressed anger affect attitude and behavior?

What are some constructive ways of expressing anger?

What would you do if you felt you were losing your mate to a competitor?

The Precocious Mother

The mother of five children stood stunned with the telephone still in her hand. It was that moment of shock before the burden of reality bears down upon us. Jim had been critically injured in an automobile accident. A thousand questions flooded her mind. Where were the car keys? Who would keep the baby? What would her homebound children do? But in the wings of her weary mind waited one question whose inevitable entrance caused the quick of her soul to quiver.

Joan was the third daughter of a black minister from upstate New York. Her father had had enormous prestige in the suburb of Albany where they lived, and all the children were spellbound by his bearing and fearful of his presence—all except Joan. She loved her father as much as any of the children, but she dared to be herself around him in ways that the others would never try. Joan had grown up in the shadow of an awesome authority and had learned to be comfortable and honest with it. She had married a young medical student and by his third year out of school, she had her fifth child. At age thirty her children were stairsteps, five in a row: ages one, two, three, four, and five. There had been times when Joan had sat in the middle of the kitchen floor and cried. But it was seldom that the children got the most of her. She gave her children as much freedom as possible so that she might win her freedom from them. Joan had learned to cope with everything with one exception, death.

"Jim is dying, come quick," the voice on the phone had said. The words danced around the core of her consciousness, toying with her mind and terrifying her soul. She locked them out of the center of herself long enough to start the car. Jim could not die. She would not let him die. He was not the immortal that her father had been but he was too tall to die. "Jim, Jim," she cried softly to herself.

When Joan reached the hospital, her husband was dead. There had been a collision at the intersection of Fifth and Main. The driver of the other car? He was drunk and uninjured. He had failed to stop at the light and had plowed into Jim on the driver's side. Jim had died from massive internal injuries.

There was a small group clustered in the hallway. When Joan saw her pastor, a tear-wet gleam came to her eye. The question would no longer remain an understudy to politeness. She wanted to know, "Does God care?" Brother Beasley was startled by her question. He felt the sting of it but he would not own up to any of his negative feelings. "Don't cry, Joan, 'all things work together for good.' "

"I don't believe you!" And there was anger in her voice.

"Now, Joan, everything's going to be all right."

"You're lying."

Beasley was speechless. He stared blankly and then looked down at the floor. He was embarrassed by his impotence.

"I don't want your pious platitudes. I asked you a question and I want an answer. Does God care that a mad drunk ruined my life? I have five children, no husband, little insurance, and no job. Does God care?" Joan exploded with a mixture of grief and anger. Then she paused and grief alone swept through her. She dropped her head and started crying. Someone put his arm around her and took her back to the car.

Brother Beasley didn't come calling the next day. Joan had a long talk with her brother who was a lawyer in Albany. Lee was as rebellious as Joan but in a nonreligious way. He cared enough to drive down to see her and she sensed his concern.

"Lee, I haven't really recovered from Daddy's death and now this," Joan shared with him. "I'm shattered. It's just not fair. That drunk was worthless and Jim had so much to offer. His practice was going great. We were going to buy a bigger house this summer. We had so many plans. He loved the kids so much. The last thing he said was to tell the baby how brilliant she was. And for some reason he didn't kiss me good-by as he usually did. He just left and now he's gone, gone forever. And the hard thing to take is that no one cares, not even God."

In a negative way Joan was asking for a positive answer. Lee was reflective for a moment. Then he began to preach. "How can a God who cares sit by and witness the slaughter of the innocent? If Jim had kissed you good-by, patted the dog, tripped over a skate, he would have missed the drunk. Anything could have delayed him five seconds, but nothing did and now he's dead. Where is God? Where is God when we flounder in our own liquid fears? If there is a God, one thing is for certain, he doesn't give a damn."

Joan knew that she would feel better if she could accept Lee's neat package of denial but the faith of her father would not let her go. The old man's life-lived faith was still very much a part of her. She remembered the police harassment when he led an early integration movement and how his courage drew interest on his faith. He was so strong yet so tender and loving. If a parishioner was hurting, he was always there and his gentle presence and warm embrace made

35

words unnecessary. She loved him for all the times he would put down his book and engulf her in his arms.

"Daddy, how come you are so strong?"

"I've been someplace," he would answer. And she remembered how he described that place in his sermons. It was a place where all was death and darkness. He called it the shadow of shadows, where wild waves broke in restless fury against a rock of ages.

"What happened there?" Joan had asked him many times. And he always answered that he didn't know. It was the valley of the shadow that the psalmist talked about and the outskirts of Jerusalem that St. Luke talked about, but her father would never describe it directly. He refused to articulate the source of his faith, but Joan had little reason to doubt the reality of his religious experience. Somehow or other she could not share his faith in the same mystical way that he did.

That afternoon the neighbors started coming by. "Don't you fret, honey, we'll help you out," Mrs. Abernathy said. And Joan knew that she would—for about two weeks. The neighbors were kind and helpful. Joan didn't know what she would do without them. However, the neighbors wouldn't pay the doctor bills and the neighbors wouldn't put five kids through school. At the dramatic moment of death everyone crowded the stage, but Joan knew that she would have to see the tragedy through alone. Did God care that her home was shattered and broken? Did God care that her only source of security would be buried this Friday afternoon? In the tick-tock mechanism of this universe was there a point of passion? Did the power that bore down upon her give a damn? Her brother was certain that it didn't and Mrs. Abernathy wasn't with it enough to answer.

Joan had no fear of storming the citadel of heaven and demanding an answer for herself, so she went for a walk.

36

Why have the shadows bivouacked at my house? Why has the curse of death plagued my door twice in one year? Why have you stolen from me the only two significant men in my life? The Lord giveth and the Lord taketh. Nonsense! Arbitrary taking is heinous and despicable. She wouldn't buy it and the pious people in her church learned quickly that Joan wasn't in the market for their platitudes.

She wanted to know where the shadows originate. She had assumed that they came from God but she began to question her assumption. What if shadows come from man, from circumstances, from fortuitous events? If so, then God was no more responsible for Jim's death than she was. Perhaps God cannot stop men from getting drunk and driving cars. She was acutely aware that God could not stop her from getting drunk if she set her stubborn will to do it.

Could a God of less than absolute power and dictatorial control be a God at all? She had always assumed that God was divine because he was the biggest boy on the block. He could exercise divinity by knocking together the heads of those who refused to recognize him. Now Joan began to question this assumption. She began to feel that God is good and loving and kind but that he is not the seat of absolute control. Shadows come from man, from fortuitous circumstances but not from God. God could be with her in the valley of the shadow because he had been there before and because the shadow was not his doing. To Lee the valley of the shadow was a denial of God, but Joan began to see it as God's arena. And she remembered a Scripture text her father often preached on, "Yea, though I walk through the valley of the shadow of death, I will fear no evil: for thou art with me" (Ps. 23:4).

When she returned home, her next-door neighbor was there. Everyone had been asking Joan what they could do for her, and for some reason this made her depression grow deeper. But her neighbor said, "Joan, would you fix me a cup of coffee?"

"Sure, just a minute." Without thinking she busied herself in the kitchen and at once she felt better. It was hard for her to put her finger on why she felt better, she just did. She was doing something for somebody else. Somebody else wanted her to do something. She was needed at the moment and for that moment that was all that mattered.

Comments

Although we cognitively recognize that death ends more marriages than divorce, there is, at most, a marginal emotional recognition of the inevitable dissolution of every marriage. We work very hard to camouflage death and we live our marriages as if it did not exist. Our culture gives us zero training in death acceptance, so we usually start our grief work as total novices.

Until recently even the church has been negligent in facing the reality of death. Over the years the church developed an elaborate game of denial which it preached, practiced, and played hard. Only in recent years have seminaries begun to train ministers to help their parishioners work through their grief experiences.

Questions

Why do we find it so difficult to face death realistically in our culture?

In what way did Joan's father communicate to her the strength of his faith?

Why did Joan find the pastor's attempts to comfort her to be platitudinous?

How would you attempt to help a friend in a similar circumstance?

What can we reasonably do to prepare ourselves to face the possible death of a spouse?

2

WIVES DON'T EITHER

The Supersalesman

Fred Gomez slumped into the overstuffed leatherette chair and stared at the floor. He had sold over a million dollars' worth of life insurance for nine consecutive years, but none of this was front and center in his consciousness. "She wants to sell the house," he forlornly said to the psychiatrist. "The house we sacrificed so much for all of these years." Fred Gomez was a fifty-year-old Mexican American who had mastered the art of selling. Watching Gomez work with a client was like watching Michelangelo paint. All his success, however, was presently overshadowed by the failure of his thirty-one-year marriage.

"How can she give up the house?"

"The house is a kind of symbol of your marriage," the psychiatrist said.

"Right now, it's the only thing holding us together. If I lose the house, I've lost Gloria for sure."

"It's hard to lose her," the psychiatrist reflected.

Gomez expended an enormous amount of physical and psychic energy to hold back the tears. He had been taught that big boys don't cry. Big boys are tough and independent. Years of conditioning had trained him not to go to anybody for help and "Don't be caught dead in a psychiatrist's office."

43

He had known for twenty years that something was wrong with his marriage, but he made two assumptions: one, that Gloria would never leave him, and two, that he could solve his own problems if he just set his head to it. He had overcome the marginal environment of Southside San Antonio and he was confident that he could work out things between Gloria and himself.

Fred Gomez was something of a counselor himself. He had talked to a hundred clients about their family problems. He could listen as well as talk and he had a storeroom of good common sense. With this combination he had helped solve dozens of marriage problems.

Gomez made many of his contacts for future sales at cocktail parties. He was a master craftsman at holding a frozen daiquiri and a warm dialogue at the same time. Fred could maneuver through a crowd, touch or talk to everyone in it and never miss a drink. When he gave a party at his house in Windcrest, it was a work of art. Fred was the youngest of five brothers and had a natural way of relating to men. If you were putting together your ideal duck hunting party, Fred would be in it. But he was a natural with women too. He could pursue a woman without her feeling manipulated or preyed upon. And the setting for Fred's creativity was always a cocktail party. He controlled a party in his Windcrest home the way a surgeon controlled his operating room. There was a chaotic movement of people and equipment, but the chaos was an illusion. Fred was in control. He knew exactly where everyone was and how much they had drunk. He always wanted them to drink more.

The change in Fred was almost imperceptible. He gained some weight. He lost a little of his charm. All of this was over the years. At rare times Fred would get drunk when he didn't intend to. Then he started drinking when he was depressed and the depression did not make a good mixer.

Fred had hit his wife only once and that had been five years ago. He had been drunk and they had gotten in a fight over who was going to take out the garbage. The next morning he apologized a hundred times. It was then that Gloria began to lose some of her respect for him. Her husband's drinking problem had slowly worsened over the last ten years of their marriage. His company had been tolerant—too tolerant. Fred had a brilliant sales and administrative record the first twenty years of his career and, out of gratitude and respect, his peers and supervisors were reluctant to confront him with his problem. And then, too, he could effectively carry out 90 percent of his job requirements.

The real problem came when Fred went home. His first stop on the way was "happy hour." This is a long-standing custom of cutting the prices of mixed drinks in half the first hour after the close of business. And at most bars happy hour is a ritual in itself. There is a fantasized spirit of community at the bar where salesmen tell war stories and relive some of the excitement of their Foreign Legion past. Salesmen can remember their traveling experiences where a real sense of community was the principal factor in their success. Fred Gomez had lots of war stories to tell. And the more he told, the more he drank. By the time he arrived home, he was plastered.

At first Gloria had enjoyed mothering her tipsy hero home from the club where he had relived a hundred selling trips in a single sitting. He would drink another Scotch or two after dinner and then drift away as old soldiers do who are fresh out of wars to fight. She began to worry about his drinking and to miss their occasional sex which stopped completely. Fred became fat. He lost his bearing and control. He would vomit on the rug and because of his weight she had to struggle to get him to bed. Their children had gone to different colleges throughout the Southwest and none of them was

45

living a life-style that Fred approved. He was infuriated because the boys wouldn't cut their hair and distrustful of his baby who had smoked marijuana. The kids were not goal-oriented as he had been and were unappreciative of the college opportunity which he had never had. When Gloria would defend their behavior, it would lead to a nasty fight.

"You always side with them," he would say as he poured himself another Scotch. Then he would drift into a negative remorse where Gloria could not touch him.

"What do you want me to do?" the psychiatrist inquired toward the end of the session.

"Save my marriage."

"I'm not sure that I can do that."

"Yeah, I know, after thirty years of messing it up, no one's going to save it overnight."

"I'm not sure that your marriage can be saved at all. Is there anything specific that you would like for me to do?"

"Yes, call Gloria and talk to her."

"She may not want to talk to me."

"I'll have her call you," Fred said as he left.

A week later Gloria did call. She saw no hope for the marriage. Because of her husband's drinking, she had lost all respect for him. "Now that the children are all through school, I just want to be me." She sounded both sad and excited at the same time. Gloria was moving into an apartment the following week.

"I know that he thinks I'm having an affair," she continued. "But that's not exactly true. I need companionship, someone to talk to without the conversation becoming a big fight or a drunken mess. I hate to leave him after all of these years but I don't want to grow old baby-sitting an alcoholic."

"Would you like to come in for a counseling session?" the psychiatrist offered.

46

"No, I don't feel there is any hope. I've made my decision and I feel comfortable with it. My husband may come back to see you."

Fred never returned and the psychiatrist often wondered what happened to him.

Comments

A big part of the American dream is private ownership of a separate dwelling. For many marriages the house is a core symbol of the relationship. The house represents many years of sacrifice and struggle. More than that, it symbolizes the relationship itself: one man committed to one woman living in a privately owned dwelling separate and apart from the rest of the world. This is seen as a magic formula for wedded bliss. The myth encourages outsiders to stay out and insiders to stay in. Anyone other than father, mother, sons and daughters are outsiders and are excluded.

Fred Gomez, like thousands of other American men, put all his chips on one bet, "If I can get her that dream house in Windcrest, she'll never leave me." When the magic didn't work he turned to booze, and the ball game was over.

There is a fantasized struggle for survival the first year or two in a new house, which ends after the lawn is in and some of the new has worn off. Then the second phase called "home improvement" emerges. This may occupy the couple's attention for several years, but the marriage is running on borrowed time if it revolves around real estate. My clinical experience indicates a large number of divorces occur twelve months to two years after a new house is purchased. The marriage is built on sand if the house becomes a core symbol.

Questions

How important is having your own home to your marriage?

What do you consider to be the advantages of living by yourselves? the disadvantages?

What relationship do you see between Fred's drinking problems and his marriage?

Do you think Fred and Gloria stayed together? Should they?

What is required to make a house a home?

The Lonely Widower

In a small town in west Tennessee, a middle-aged couple was cuddled in front of their one extravagant luxury, a mammoth wood-burning fireplace. There was no way that Janet and Peter could afford the extra thousand dollars that it cost, so they had borrowed the money from Janet's father and had indulged themselves with a nostalgic dream of yesteryear when stockings were hung and books were read by a roaring fire. They had made love in front of the fireplace many times. Afterward, they reminisced about their courting days when they would roll up in a blanket by an open fire in the woods back of Janet's house.

"Peter, this Christmas I want to tell you how beautiful you are."

"No, no. I can't stand it." He laughed with a mild embarrassment.

"Be serious and listen to me. You're warm and loving and kind. And your body is as strong as your heart is tender. Your shoulders are broad and wide and rippling with muscles." As she talked, her long, sensitive fingers traced an endless nonverbal message across his brow and down his neck and around his chest. He was drunk with her touch and madly in love with his wife of fifteen years.

Janet Miles was the middle daughter of a family of five girls and she had that grace and charm that only sisters can teach each other. Her personality was radiant and her smile infectious. When she walked into a room, she spread germs of ecstasy. Women were seldom turned off by her classic beauty because she had learned so early to relate well to her older and younger sisters. Her father, who was a high school math teacher, never fully knew what a genius of charm and grace his middle daughter was, but he was a devoted family man and Janet had a good relationship with him. She could tease him and feel safe that his response would be as warm as her approach. Janet moved toward people with a joyful spontaneity. She had never known rejection.

Peter was an assistant professor of art in Martin, Tennessee. He was the happiest poor man east of the Mississippi. There was little chance for promotion in his department, and Peter had known this when he took the job. But he wanted to live in Martin and he wanted to teach art. He cared very little about promotion as long as Janet was happy. She was his wealth, riches, and reason to be. Janet had deep roots in central west Tennessee and wanted to live there, so Peter turned down a chance to teach at Memphis State, which would have meant an associate professor position which is one notch above assistant professor. When he married Janet, Peter traded his ambition for a leisurely life of art and love.

Peter and Janet came from remarkably similar backgrounds. They were children of high school teachers. Their mothers were artists who had sold paintings at local art galleries and had taught their children an appreciation of art early in life. Peter was the youngest of three boys and was flooded with the attention and affection of the entire family. His parents were in their early forties when he was born. They had wanted a girl but they loved him dearly from the moment they first saw him. Janet's father had wanted a boy but her dark-black hair and beautiful complexion had stolen his heart from the outset. Both sides of the family were Southern Baptist and their fathers had been deacons in west Tennessee Baptist churches. They also had been strict disciplinarians. Janet's father would chuckle when he told about a bedtime experience.

"Daddy, will you get me a glass of milk?"

"No, dear, you had some milk before you went to bed."

Thirty minutes later.

"Daddy, will you get me a glass of milk?"

"I told you no, Janet. If you bother me one more time, I'm going to get up and spank you."

A half hour later.

"Daddy, when you get up to spank me, would you mind getting me a glass of milk?"

Peter and Janet had worked very hard at being open and honest with each other. When Peter's mother died, Janet said that she knew how he must feel and Peter had confronted her with the fact that she didn't know how it felt to lose a mother that she was very close to. So when Peter's father died, Janet struggled very hard to get with his feelings and avoided the platitudes that everyone else passed out. As a result of years of honesty they had learned to enjoy each other's company enormously; consequently, they had not cultivated many close friends. They just did not play games with each other and found their game-playing peers in the college community to be unbearable bores. They enjoyed their evenings at home reading poetry to each other or listening to classical music. When their tastes in literature or music differed, they had learned how to negotiate their differences and reach a point of mutual sharing. When they did go out to social events they were well received, but they did not choose to go out very often.

Janet never became pregnant and they talked about adoption on several occasions. They made contact with a social service agency but they failed to follow it up.

"To tell the truth, I'm not particularly anxious to share you even with a son," Peter had confessed. "I know that this sounds terribly selfish, but there are so many beautiful things that I can do with you if you don't have to wash diapers and sterilize bottles." Janet discussed her natural motherly instincts and was able to work through them without feeling deprived by her barrenness. All her sisters had children, so there was little pressure from her parents for grandchildren. Janet felt her immortality was in her paintings and Peter quickly agreed. They didn't sell well now, but many of the great artists had not been recognized in their lifetimes. Janet felt that she would be remembered through her art. This was not the same as leaving behind your own flesh and blood, but she had poured her soul into her paintings and she was sure that they would survive.

Janet was taking a shower when she first felt the lump in her breast. For two weeks she said nothing about it but then she began to worry.

"Janet, something's been bothering you this week," Peter said and she exploded into tears.

"I've got a lump in my right breast and I'm afraid to go to the doctor."

The next day Peter went with her to the college physician. Two days later the tests came back—positive. After two operations and five months in the hospital, Janet died at the age of forty-three. Peter Miles's entire life ended the moment she left him. He was holding her hand and could feel her slipping away. He begged her not to leave him, but at five thirty one Tuesday afternoon she did.

Peter lived in a daze for six months after she died. He placed himself under house arrest and sentenced himself to a nonexistence. He would sleep with her unframed paintings rolled up in his arms and, on occasion, he would wrap them with a pair of her old pajamas. He would moan her name in a magical ritual of empty expectancy. Janet did not hear. She did not come back.

The following fall, Peter forced himself to return to school. He lectured in a robot manner, and in art lab he would say to every student, "That looks fine, very good," even if the painting was terrible. Several professors invited him over to their homes for dinner and in other ways they tried to make contact with him, but he politely and firmly refused every offer. Both of Peter's older brothers had moved to New England and he would see neither of them between Janet's death and his own. His only trips outside the city were to Janet's grave and to the cemetery where his parents were buried. After two years of this nonexistence, Peter was called in by the head of his department. "Peter, I hate to have to tell you this, but the quality of your work has fallen off enormously and if this pattern continues, I will have to terminate your contract next year. If there is anything my wife and I can do, I want you to let me know and we'll make every effort to help you out of this depression."

Peter resigned on the spot. No one could change his mind. He went home to die and six months later, he did. His body was not found until eight days after his heart attack. The neighbors stood around the front yard as Peter was placed in the hearse. They all felt a little guilty about their noninvolvement with him at the time of his death.

"He had stopped the newspaper last month, so there wasn't much way to tell that he was even sick," one neighbor said.

"He seldom received mail, so his mailbox wasn't stuffed either."

"Who found the body?"

"The people from the telephone company came to disconnect his phone."

"That's really sad," a lady said and everyone was quiet for a long time.

"Anyone know what he did with all those paintings?"

"The telephone man said there wasn't a painting in the house and it looked like someone had built a big fire in the living room fireplace. It was all covered with soot and there were some charred picture frames that had not completely burned."

"And his wife was a pretty good painter too."

"Oh, well, the Lord giveth and the Lord taketh," a woman said. No one felt like adding anything after that.

There were four people at Peter's funeral: the minister, the undertaker, one brother, and the head of the art department. The service was concluded with "Blessed be the name of the Lord." They all thanked the minister for the beautiful service and each went home to his own tight little circle of security.

Comments

Marriage at its very best can be tragic. Death can steal away the most beautiful relationship imaginable. Most men, including myself, do not want to dwell very long on the fact that this happens every day in a thousand homes in a hundred cities. No couple lives "happily ever after," but the current marriage myth implies that they do.

I believe that the institution of marriage can be changed to lessen the blow of the terminal separation. Peter and Janet could have chosen to share their lives and economic involvement with another couple. A quartet is less vulnerable than a dyad. Two or three couples who are courageous enough to share their lives can grow old together and be less traumatized by the inevitable loss of individual members. This would not require communal living but it does require joint economic involvement.

Questions

What was the basic cause of Peter's tragic ending?

Why were his concerned colleagues and associates unable to help him?

What real involvements do you have with persons other than your spouse?

How are lasting and meaningful friendships established?

Would joint ownership of a camper, a summer cottage, or a boat add a new dimension to your life?

The Vice-President's Daughter

Jo Ann McDowell was the sister of three older brothers, each of whom saw himself as her protector.

"Look out for your little sister," their mother had repeated until it was a part of their mental makeup. They did. They were overprotective in a way that parents could never be. Jo Ann loved it, until she left for college. One bright fall day in September, she became an orphan. Her parents were still very much alive and Daddy was still vice-president of a bank in Houston, Texas, but there weren't any big brothers around to take care of Jo Ann. She would not have survived if she had not been brilliant. She learned quickly that college professors would take a big-brother role if she made them look good, and she was a professional at making older men look good.

In the middle of her senior year Jo Ann felt the same panic. Was there anyone she could lean on when she graduated? She had a teacher's certificate and was assured a job, but there wouldn't be any college professors at Oak Grove Elementary School. It was about this time that Jo Ann met Wayne. He was bagging groceries at the store where she went to buy midnight snacks. Wayne was the older brother of two younger sisters and could spot a "little sister" halfway across the supermarket. Jo Ann was a walking invitation. He carried her bag to the car. It was locked and the keys were inside.

"What'll I do?"

"Just hold this bag and I'll get a coat hanger."

Wayne had rescued a dozen locked-out ladies but never before had he enjoyed it so much. Distressed women were his specialty. He opened Jo Ann's car with a flourish.

"How can I ever thank you enough?"

"Your telephone number."

She refused to give it to him but she checked out at his counter for the next three months. Two weeks after she graduated, they were married.

Jo Ann's parents were petrified. Wayne had dropped out of school after his second semester and although he said he planned to go back, Jo Ann's folks were not convinced. They were openly skeptical.

"Jo Ann, I wouldn't be so worried if it wasn't so obvious that he enjoys bagging groceries."

"He'll go back to school."

Her mother was doubtful but even if he did, she did not want Jo Ann to have to finance her husband's education. "Don't count on your father putting him through school," she warned. Jo Ann's brothers were unanimous in their opposition to the marriage. They had not raised their little sister to marry a bag boy.

Wayne was not ignorant about all of this, but there was no way he was going back to school with only Jo Ann's salary to support them. School had been a bad experience for him and he didn't relish a quick return. He was being pulled in six different directions when he walked into the Army recruiter's office. On the way to the supermarket, he would turn left at a big sign that said, "The modern Army wants to join you." Wayne didn't know why this sign caught his attention, but he mumbled under his breath, "It's for damn sure that nobody else wants to join me." The recruiter carefully explained all the benefits and the many options. Wayne could receive four years of GI college payments for two years of service. He could enlist for his choice of duty stations.

"You mean I can choose my first assignment?" Wayne sounded unbelieving.

"After completion of basic training and your advanced individual training."

"How long does all of that take?"

"About four months."

"I find this too good to believe. I've heard stories about how recruiters promise you everything."

"I'll put everything I say in writing."

Wayne was a little worried about the physical exam. During his senior year in high school he had developed a malignancy that required minor surgery. He was afraid that if he told the doctor about it he would flunk his physical. He wanted those college benefits so badly that he decided to keep quiet about his medical problem. If the doctor noticed the small scar, he would tell him about the malignancy. If he didn't, he would keep his mouth shut. Wayne took his exam late in the afternoon and the doctor was dog-tired. He never saw the scar. Wayne took a deep breath when he walked out. Two naked young men were still standing in line to see the doctor. "If you're warm, you'll pass," Wayne said to the first one with that tone of the experienced veteran.

Wayne had never known that time could be structured so tightly as it was in basic training. He was too busy to dwell long on the fact that Jo Ann was pregnant and would have to miss a year of teaching. He had figured that the best way to keep Jo Ann was to keep her pregnant. "Few pregnant women file for divorce," someone had told him. But after basic training was over, Wayne paused long enough to reflect upon what he was doing with his life. Although he missed Jo

Ann something terrible, he was really pleased to be planning his life apart from her family. Jo Ann's father could take his bank and cram it. For two years in the green machine he would have four years of subsidized schooling.

Back home in Houston, Jo Ann was not feeling so well. Army privates had little more status in her family than bag boys. Her oldest brother was a major in the Air Force, so Jo Ann didn't brag a lot about Wayne doing well in basic training. She didn't even tell the family when he made Pfc. Jo Ann eagerly joined him when he received his first duty assignment at Fort Bragg, North Carolina. Fayetteville, North Carolina, is a town that has consistently refused to enter the twentieth century while at the same time it has lost the charm of the nineteenth. It is a city without a century. It also is lacking in adequate low-income housing. Jo Ann was appalled at what $150 would rent in Fayetteville. On Wayne's salary and with her seven months pregnant, they couldn't afford to spend any more. Thank God the baby could be born in the hospital on the post.

Wayne's disillusionment with the military started when he flunked out of jump school. He had really wanted that extra pay for jump duty. Although his old high school ailment began to bother him on the long daily runs, he was afraid to go on sick call and get treatment. If the Army learned about his malignancy, it would discharge him for fraudulent enlistment and he would lose his GI benefits. During all these problems, Wayne was less attentive to Jo Ann's needs than he had formerly been back in Texas. He was aware of this but he knew how to keep her pregnant and he was convinced that she would never leave him as long as she was in a motherly way.

After two years, Wayne was faced with the one thing he liked least—a big decision. Jo Ann wanted him to stay in the Army. She had two children, little desire to return to teaching, and a deep fear of Wayne's illness returning while they were struggling through three years of school. Even though she didn't like being married to a Spec 4, she had found a feeling of security in the Army and she didn't want to let it go. Wayne was disillusioned with the Army and wanted out.

"Please, Wayne, I've never begged you before but I'm begging you now. Don't get out." Her tears were a waterfall and behind the tears was a little girl who was very scared.

"A man has to live his own life," Wayne told himself as he processed out of the Army. The doctor failed to see the scar at his discharge physical and Wayne was a happy man when he gave Fort Bragg "the finger" and told Fayetteville good-by.

A month later, Wayne was back at school in Austin, Texas. Jo Ann had asked to stay with her folks in Houston until Wayne could find an apartment they could afford. Getting back to the books wasn't easy for Wayne, but after his fourth week he was convinced that he could do it. It was a Friday afternoon, and he was working on algebra when the doorbell rang. The man at the door didn't say a word; he just held out a long envelope.

"What's this?"

The man remained speechless. Wayne opened the envelope and could tell that it contained a legal document.

"Listen, man, what the hell is this?"

"Divorce papers."

Wayne slumped in the doorway and the speechless man walked away. Although Wayne made a dozen trips to Houston and wrote a bushel of letters that were never answered, nothing he could say would change Jo Ann's mind. By the time the divorce was final, Wayne was too discouraged to even ask for visitation rights, a decision that he later regretted.

Comments

Martin Luther is reported to have said, "God gave women big hips because he intended for them to stay home and sit on them." In the sixteenth century a man could get away with this degree of chauvinism, but in the latter half of the twentieth century he is gambling with his personal well-being if he tries. There are many men who do. "Keep her barefoot and pregnant" has been altered only to the point of shodding her feet. There are bright, intelligent men whose only strategy for keeping their wives is to make their stomachs big and their cradles full. Praise God, the strategy doesn't work so well anymore. The women's liberation movement has been an exercise in courage. An oppressed gender is saying, "Enough!"

In the recent years of my clinical experience I have seen an increasing number of wives who are not willing to exist on the vicarious drippings from their husband's career. They are demanding that their essential emotional needs be met. When their basic needs go unfulfilled, they are less reluctant than before to leave their husband and search elsewhere. The "life sentence" concept of marriage among American women is being repealed by women who vote with their feet.

Questions

What did Wayne and Jo Ann seek in a marriage partner?
In what ways was Wayne a male chauvinist?
How have you encountered sexism in your own marriage?
Would you think a marriage worth preserving in which one partner feels used by the other?
What would a marriage be like that allowed personal fulfillment as well as sexual satisfaction?

3

And
It Would Be
Boring If
They Did

THE RAT RACERS

Judy Clements was a slender, beautiful, intense, competitive, thirty-two-year-old woman. She was custom-made for idolizing. "Let me tell you about my date" was easy to say when the coed involved was Judy. In college she had made the best of grades and had dated the most attractive boys. "I simply want the best of everything," she boldly admitted. "I won't settle for second best in anything." In reality her college degree proved only two things: one, she was capable of learning, and two, she was willing to put up with endless trivia. Judy wanted A's on her transcript, and if learning trivia was required, she would do it. She did. She graduated cum laude and was married the first week in June.

Fred Clements was not Mr. America but he was intelligent, athletic, and ambitious. He also had a degree in accounting. Fred, who was neither as intense nor as competitive as Judy, wanted basically the same kind of life that she did —two kids, a nice car, a big house, and a prestigious job. He wasn't picky as long as he got the best. And like Judy he was willing to work as hard as necessary to get the upper-middle-class life that he wanted.

Fred and Judy had met at a summer church camp and both had said to themselves about the other, "That's what I want."

Since neither of them was open enough to admit it, they both played "hard to get" while pursuing each other at full speed. There is a certain expectation for people to act religious at church camps even though it is well known that the basic reason churches have them is to ensure that Baptist boys marry Baptist girls and that Methodist boys marry Methodist girls. So Fred and Judy both sang, "Every day with Jesus is sweeter than the day before," while each anxiously checked which boy or girl the other was sitting by. Although they were much more concerned about Friday night's date than they were with the sweetness of Jesus, they played the religious game and waited for that moment of magic when they would be alone and deeply in love.

It came that summer and many times later but it never lasted. The magic always wore off. Fred's father had said love never lasts, either you marry the girl or you forget her. Either way, the emotional intoxication comes to an abrupt end. Fred never believed him until his second anniversary. Judy was pregnant and sick and disgusting. She had never wanted sex very often, it took her a week to have her period, a week to get ready for it, and a week to get over it. Fred was fortunate to have one good week a month. Now that she was pregnant, she was as sexy as an angry rhinoceros. She was too sick in the mornings and too tired at night. But the magic would return when the baby came, and eight months was not too long to wait. Fred bought a camera and by the time the baby was born he had mastered photography as only a parent can.

The baby was fun for the first five months. Fred and Judy were both elated over their little boy. They took a thousand pictures. Fred saw all kinds of signs of superior intelligence and Judy saw leadership qualities that would take him beyond state government. But it is hard to fantasize greatness when your kid has diarrhea and the washing machine is broken and you're up to your elbows in dirty diapers. No one takes pictures of dirty bottoms. Judy squinched up her nose and dreamed of the beautiful house they were going to build.

The house they wanted was out of their reach, so they structured their time in shopping for a car. They bought all the magazines and attended the auto shows with all the fervor they had once expended on church camp. Neither of them was satisfied with cheap American imitations. They wanted the real thing. Maybe a Ferrari or the big BMW. Fred liked the Mercedes-Benz 280SL and Judy was partial to a blue Alfa Romeo. Fred had not been so excited since he bought a Canon camera. They trained themselves to feel superior to Austin Healey owners and they wouldn't look at a Triumph. They would sooner have joined a Pentecostal church. After two years of shopping they bought a year-old Mercedes Coupe. Fred toyed with the idea of racing it, but Judy asked him what he was out to prove and, after checking the insurance rates for racing, he decided that the whole idea was childish. Fred could get his goodies just driving to work. There was a feeling of power that came from the responsiveness of the vehicle. The acceleration was intoxicating. This excitement lasted for five months. After that, traffic jams were traffic jams and bottlenecks were bottlenecks. The only real difference five months later was that car repairs were more expensive. A responsive car can help you forget an unresponsive wife for only so long Fred told a friend at work.

Home hunting and house worshiping were a larger part of their lives. It was a bigger project and a more efficient camouflage to the drabness of their daily lives. If either one had stopped the rat race long enough to say, "Hey, I'm bored," they might have gotten a handle on what was wrong, but the monthly payments were always just large enough to keep them extremely busy. They studied blueprints for sixteen months and searched three counties until they found an inspiring piece of real estate. Although the land alone exhausted all of their savings, they just were not content with the typical suburban dwelling. Judy wanted something she could spend ten years landscaping.

Fred borrowed the money from his parents to make the down payment on the house. They expected him to repay it, so he found it necessary to moonlight with a weekend job. Working seven days a week left him exhausted, but exhaustion helps to mask many unfulfilled needs. Home improvement does too. Fred would work for hours in the summer on patios and driveways while Judy planted flowers and set out bushes. They were too tired at the end of the day to do anything other than collapse and remain unconscious until the rat race began all over the next day. In the winter there was always the attic to insulate and to floor. They wanted to expand their house to a magical 2,500 square feet. With one boy they had little need for this amount of floor space, but there was status in having a really big house. Although there was enough room for two or three families, the idea of sharing their house never entered their minds. It was theirs alone. They had worked for it. It had met their needs. More accurately it had camouflaged some of their basic needs, but they were not in touch with this.

Three years after they moved in they began to get bored. The lawn was all in and the grass that they had thought would never get started was now growing faster than Fred wanted it to. At first he could fantasize the lawn as his farm. It was a little over an acre in size and just large enough for him to maintain the myth that he was a frontiersman struggling to clear the land and survive in the wilderness. The myth had blown away and now mowing was a bore. The trees which had been so romantic and magical the first two years were now just something to mow around. All the bushes were growing and all the flowers were blooming and all their sinuses were aching. Their ultimate idol was beginning to crack.

Judy and Fred had the best of everything for an upper-middle-class couple, but when the magic wore off they almost became frantic. A promotion at Fred's job provided some salt for their tasteless lives, then the excitement of this petered out too. They tried the club routine but they couldn't afford the country club dues, so tennis and bridge were the focus of their lives for a couple of summers. Both were competitive enough to enjoy the excitement of winning, but winning in a bush league can soon get old. It is no fun beating the same people over and over again. When they tried staying at home and sitting around the fireplace they found that they had a limited number of topics to discuss. They had sailed these courses so often that the waters were weary with their sameness. Strangely enough, to admit that something was wrong was taboo. There was an unwritten contract between them that they would never admit their boredom. The contract called for them always to try something else, but the something else was limited to the very small box they lived in. They were running a maze they had not created in a laboratory they had not designed. Worst of all, when they became bored they had a tendency to blame themselves.

Comments

"If you win the rat race, you're still a rat," a friend said to me one afternoon at a point in my life when I was intent on staying a step ahead of my peers. The race was fun back then, but eventually the circular sameness of the track got old and in my suburban boredom I began to ask some questions.

I wanted to know who designed the track and why it went the way it did. My clients were as bored as I was. They were searching for solutions too. The traditional answer was to try harder, run faster, but this didn't work. The faster you run on a circular track the sooner you see the same things again. And if you win, you are simply a bored counselor who is one step ahead of his bored clients. It was at this point in my life that I began to ask questions about the structure of the institution of marriage. Most of these questions are rattling around in the case story of Fred and Judy.

Questions

To what extent does the story of Fred and Judy parallel your own life?

Contrast the American dream of getting ahead with the New Testament concept of the abundant life.

What are the real roots of the boredom in Fred and Judy's life together?

What practical suggestions can you offer for changing such a life-style?

Are you likely to follow your own advice? Why or why not?

THE HONEST TEEN-AGER

Jeff Godfrey grew up in a home where the *National Geographic* had been banned. He had been caught looking at pictures of bare-breasted native women. Until he married, these were the only nude female figures he had ever seen. Jeff's parents never stated their personal convictions about nudity, but they would say things like, "We don't look at pictures like that in this house." There was an ill-defined deity that hovered over his home, and his parents were ambassadors who interpreted its will. Although Jeff hated this amorphous puritan pharisee which his parents worshiped, he wasn't allowed to express any negative feeling about it or his parents. Negative feelings could only be directed at enemies and when Jeff's folks didn't have any convenient enemies, they invented some. Life was so much simpler for them during World War I. They liked to be told whom they were supposed to hate. At those times when there were no national enemies to hate, their restrictions on Jeff were most severe.

Jeff married a Catholic girl named Pauline Stevens. Jeff's Protestant parents were much displeased with his choice of a Catholic for his spouse, but they learned to love Pauline quickly—she was as uptight as they were. Pauline had attended a Catholic school where the girls were not allowed to

71

wear patent leather shoes because if they did, the boys would be tempted to look up their dresses through the reflection in their shiny shoes.

Jeff and Pauline had a good marriage. They were not allowed to have a bad one. Good people have good marriages; Jeff and Pauline were good people, so they did what they were supposed to, they had a good marriage. And if they had not had children, they might have been able to maintain the myth of their marital bliss. Their youngest daughter refused to be brainwashed.

"I don't want this 'That's not the way we do it in this family' nonsense. Just tell me what you don't want," Terri had exploded when her father would try to interpret for some unseen family deity. Terri inherited a long-dormant strain of courage from a great-grandfather who fought Indians on the frontier. She would not accept the family litanies of the past if they didn't make sense for San Diego in 1971. And much of what her parents had accepted in their Midwestern upbringing did not make sense in San Diego. Among Terri's friends premarital sex was as natural as water running downhill. They simply did not question the morality of it. Terri felt that her parents would never change their sex views, so she did not think it necessary to fight this particular battle with them. By the time she was eighteen, she had sex when it seemed appropriate to her.

One fall morning, while Terri was at school, Pauline decided to clean up her daughter's room. Terri's room normally looked like the result of a direct hit by an enemy artillery barrage. This particular morning, her mother wanted to clean it up, thoroughly. And in the process she found what she feared. In the bottom left-hand drawer she found an appointment slip to the Free Clinic. To Pauline, the Free Clinic was synonymous with VD. When Terri came home that afternoon, the inquisition was in full flower.

"How could you do this to us? After all we've done for you. How could you disgrace us like this?"

"I don't have the foggiest idea what you are talking about."

"What is this?" Pauline held up the appointment slip like it was the severed head of John the Baptist.

"Where did you get that?"

"I was cleaning up your room."

"Mother, you have no right to be going through my things."

"Young lady, don't tell me what I have a right to do in my own house."

"Have it your own way, Mother. If I have to leave to get some privacy, I'll move out tomorrow."

Pauline was afraid that this might happen. Terri was in her first year of college and had wanted to move to an apartment with some girl friends. Her boyfriend wanted her to move in with him.

"Terri, all I want to know is if you're sick or something. Why did you go to the clinic?" Her mother quickly retreated.

"Well, if you must know, I had an IUD put in last month." Terri paused and the silence was too much for both of them. "I just don't want to get pregnant, that's all."

"Darling, you're not married. Why do you need protection when you're not married?"

"Mother, this is not the Dark Ages. This is San Diego 1971. All my friends have sex." Terri paused. There was no easy way to tell her mother. "And I do too."

Pauline was crying. Her rigid Victorian past could not assimilate the avalanche. "Terri, we worked so hard to bring you up right. Your father and I took you to church every Sunday and now, Terri, how could you do this to us?"

"Mother, you and Daddy have always wanted to suffocate me with your do's and don'ts. I'm eighteen and this has just got to stop."

"Don't you think we love you? Don't you think I'm concerned about this because I want you to be happy?" Pauline was certain she could gain an advantage if she could shift the argument to an emotional level where she could call in the gods of her puritan past. "Don't you think I want what is best for you?"

"No!" It was the most forceful syllable the young woman had ever uttered. "If you want to know what I think, I'll tell you. You and Daddy are overly concerned about me because you are bored with each other."

"Darling, don't say things like that."

"I just did." Terri refused to budge. "The past five years you've been able to forget how dull your own life is by meddling with mine. But I'm not going to let it continue. I've got my own life to live and, Mother, it may be different from the way you and Dad live yours."

The human animal has an uncanny ability to deny the existential reality of the moment. Pauline refused to believe that her daughter meant what she was saying.

"Terri, I've made an appointment with Dr. Butler for three o'clock. We're going down and have that thing taken out. Now I don't want any fuss. I just want it out."

Terri stared in disbelief. She started to say something, but instead she turned and ran to her room. She pulled the suitcases from the back of her closet and in a ritual of rebellion banged them on the bed. It took her fifteen minutes to pack and in that fifteen minutes, she was born again.

"Thank God your father is driving up. Maybe he can talk some sense into your head."

"What's going on?" Jeff Godfrey wanted to know.

"Terri's leaving us," her mother half sobbed. "I learned

she has an IUD and when I asked her to take it out, she started packing her suitcase."

"Mother, you didn't ask. You demanded."

"Terri, you know how much we love you. We only want what is best for you." Her father pursued a worn path that had never worked, but hope springs eternal.

"I know how much you want to interfere with my life."

"Terri, it's only for your own good."

"I don't believe that. I know that you care about me but your suffocating interference is because you are bored and don't have anything else to do. I'm tired of being the scapegoat in this family." She took a deep breath. "I want to live my own life and if I have to work my way through college, I'll do it."

Her father had never felt more impotent. His daughter's maturity could have been a reason for rejoicing, but his inner system of balance was threatened by Terri's departure. Would there be someone else for them to pick on when Terri was gone? Jeff Godfrey was not honest enough consciously to ask this but deep within his psychic system the question was bouncing up and down.

Terri, with a suitcase in each hand, was crying when she kissed the tight, taut lips of her mother, but she had mustered the courage to break out of a box and it felt really good to be free.

Comments

There is increasing clinical evidence that parents are translating their boredom with each other into an overconcern for their teen-age children. I have counseled numerous parents who were taxi drivers for their teen-agers. They spent two or more hours a day driving their children to various activities. Ninety percent of their conversation was focused upon their children. This is the behavior of adults who have lost interest in their own lives and try to draw vicarious satisfaction from the life of their teen-ager.

Terri was able to break away from the suffocating restrictions of her family, but many teen-agers are unable to do this. When they don't make a successful break with their primary family, the resultant life pattern is punctuated with pain. Teen-agers who assert their autonomy and affirm their own individual existence have a life posture in which they can continue to love and appreciate their parents.

Questions

Why is there often tension and misunderstanding between parents and teen-agers?

To what extent do you hold the same moral standards that prevailed in the home where you were raised?

Why are the well-meaning efforts of parents to train their children so often resented?

How can you teach children to be responsible and self-reliant?

How can you prepare yourself to let them go?

The Faithful Husband

Herbert and Martha had quarreled their way through thirty-five years of marriage. They hated each other at the end of their fifteenth year and they hated each other at the end of their thirty-fifth year. Their first ten years were an uneasy truce. The children were time-consuming and Herbert worked at a second job, so they didn't spend much time together. One afternoon a friend asked Martha if she had ever considered divorcing Herbert and she replied: "No, never divorce. I considered murdering him several times but never divorce."

"How come?" the friend wanted to know.

"Well, it's lonely by yourself and we don't go to Mass now, but we were both raised Catholic and there's just a bad feeling about living in sin and all of that, you know."

The friend didn't know but she said yes anyway. Martha, fat and fiftyish, seldom had a listening ear that was interested in her marriage, so she shared some things that she had not unearthed in several years.

"Herbert was a bookkeeper and we lived in Mississippi," she began with a deep sigh as if it was laborious just to remember it. "He would never have made it, if I hadn't pulled him through. I had to raise the kids and I had to make

77

the money. A bookkeeper's salary back in those days was nothing. I even kept the checkbook." Martha stopped for a moment, took a deep breath, and primed her internal psychic apparatus for a machine-gun attack on Herbert. When she set her mind to it, she could do it well.

"Couldn't he do anything?" Her friend's question was all the push she needed.

"No, nothing. He never has been able to do anything except to criticize me. You know he didn't like my teeth and, stupid me, I went to a dentist and had a bridge made. Where's my picture?" Martha fingered through her purse and pulled out a worn and damaged portrait of herself prior to her dental work. "Now I ask you, were those bad-looking teeth?"

"I don't see a thing wrong with them," her friend said.

"Well, Herbert did. He bitched and he nagged until I went to the dentist and had all that pain and pulling. But nothing would please him. 'Looks artificial,' he said. I could have killed him. And would you believe he never helped around the house when I was having all that work done."

"Just like a man."

"Let me show you something," Martha said as she pulled up her dress and exposed her upper thigh where there was a small bruise the size of a quarter.

"Your husband did that? I don't see how you can stay with him."

"It's not easy, let me tell you that. But he couldn't make it without me. He's a little lost boy when I'm not around. I have to make him wear a tie when we go out to eat. I've told him over and over: 'Herbert, just don't embarrass me. That's all I ask of you.' But he'll do it every time. I'm ashamed to be seen in public with him."

Martha's friend was beginning to get bored. Every time she started to change the subject, Martha would increase her pace like a mile runner who refuses to be overtaken.

"Last week I smelled tobacco on his breath," Martha continued. "Nothing makes me madder than for Herbert to smoke behind my back. I have told him over and over again that I would not tolerate tobacco but he'll slip out like the kid that he is and smoke behind my back. He knows that it's not good for him but he'll do it just to spite me."

"Make him promise."

"I do but his promises are as worthless as he is. He promised me two months ago that he would never smoke again and you know what I did? I called up his office and asked the man whose desk is next to Herbert's if he was smoking. And you know what? Herbert had that guy lie to me. I could tell by his voice that he was lying. Herbert lies and lies and now he's even got the fellows at the office lying for him."

Martha shifted her weight to the bruised leg without displaying any sign of discomfort. Her friend was feverishly trying to devise a polite exit from Martha's verbal entanglement, but Martha had a way of not letting a person escape. She had learned to force you to either passively accept her or rudely embarrass her, and few people were willing to do the latter. Out of desperation Herbert had learned to do the latter. He would store up his anger bit by bit until like steam in a boiler, the whole thing would explode. He would then push her or slap her and run for the nearest exit before she could hook him with her battered-wife chant of woe and anguish. A marriage counselor had once said to him, "I couldn't live with her." But Herbert knew of no way to make a permanent escape. After three or four drinks at a local bar, he always went back. Going back was his self-punishment for having been so beastly as to beat his wife. The most sadistic priest in Christendom could not have created a more difficult penance.

Martha sensed her friend's struggle to come up for air, so she pushed her back with a fresh atrocity. "And just yesterday he promised to paint the bathroom. He hasn't touched it. Hasn't even bought the paint. So I'll have to go to the hardware and I'll have to pick out the color, buy the paint and stick it under his nose."

"Did Herbert ever step out on you? I mean with another woman?" the friend interjected, hoping for something a little juicier than the battle of the bathroom.

"Never! He doesn't have the guts to. Herbert wouldn't dare. I can never count on him for anything except to keep his fly zipped." Martha hesitated, then lowered her voice. "I can't even get him interested in me. I put on a frilly night-gown and he just ignores me."

The friend, sensing a rare occasion to go on the offensive, said, "Maybe he's sleeping with someone else."

"Not Herbert, the gutless wonder. Besides, he knows that I wouldn't stand for it. We haven't drifted that far from the church." Martha wrinkled her nose as the thought of her husband's sole virtue was as displeasing to her as his impotence. "The only good thing that I can say about Herbert is that he's faithful. He knows that he had better be."

"I really must be going," the friend said. Martha had paused when she realized that she had been sucked into a defensive posture. Quite anxious in any interaction if she lost control of it, she had learned to hold control by offensively attacking anyone who would not join her in berating an absent third party. She carefully trained people to join her tirades lest they become the target of them.

"No, you can't go now. I've just started on Herbert. I haven't even told you about the time he beat me within an inch of my life when I was pregnant with Elsie."

The friend sighed and the staccato of Martha's machine gun droned on and on.

Comments

Martha is a thoroughgoing bitch. More concerned with the color of the bathroom than with the quality of her relationship with Herbert, she has enough ego strength to run General Motors but lacks the sensitivity of an angry water buffalo. She trains people to cringe. Her husband's faithfulness is cringe-oriented. But Herbert is not without responsibility for the dysfunctional marriage, for he constantly undermines and sabotages the best efforts of Martha. He is a professional insurgent.

Questions

What holds this marriage together?
Is it worth preserving?
In what ways is Herbert unfaithful to Martha?
In what ways is she unfaithful to him?
How would you define faithfulness in marriage?

4
Marriage Is an Institution That Doesn't Always Work

THE PREGNANT SENIOR

Lisa Langford owned Jackson Jr.-Sr. High School. You could tell it by the way she walked down the halls. Her grades weren't all that good, but she had an unshakable rapport with the teachers. She got along with the administration even better. And, strangely enough, this professional teacher's pet also related well to her peers. In the vernacular of Jackson High she was stacked, which meant that she had a very good figure. This didn't hurt her any, and her sparkling personality was a sure plus in her favor.

Lisa was into everything: the chorus, the clubs, the basketball team. She played basketball like she walked the halls—possessively. She owned the court. She could shoot with either hand equally well. Her hook shot with her left hand was unbelievable and Lisa knew it. Her concentration was intense, but the moment she released the ball she had the unusual ability to relax and enjoy the shot. She could laugh and cry and grieve along with the crowd. She was good, she knew she was good, and she let you know she was good. But her ability to relax and enjoy herself helped her to get away with an immense amount of self-indulgence.

Lisa was especially good in a program designed by the

principal to deal with social problems in the school. The heart of the program was a series of therapy group sessions in which students could ventilate their feelings in the presence of their peers. It was a student-helping-student program that worked so well that the principal and his staff had to cope with few of the normal disciplinary problems. Lisa was a leader in this program and was particularly good at leading groups. She moved toward her peers with less hesitation than a streetwalker. And she had no hesitation about saying: "You're as phony as a three-dollar bill. I would like it a lot better if you would be real for a moment and let me know where you're coming from." She had an unusual ability to confront in kindness. Her skills in counseling had been noticed by the principal and her English teacher, both of whom encouraged her to think about a career in this field.

Lisa had applied for admission at the state university and although her B grades were not the best, she had done well on the college board examination and felt sure she would be accepted. Her principal owed her a favor and had written a friend on the board of regents. Lisa knew exactly what she wanted to do with her life and was moving in that direction.

Jackson High also had an outstanding football team whose star running back dated Lisa on a regular basis. He had pressured her to go steady, but she had consistently refused. He also had pressured Lisa to have sex with him. This she also refused until one night Jack was over and her parents were gone. One thing led to another. It was brief, awkward, and somewhat painful for Lisa. Two months later she knew that she was pregnant. And for all her togetherness Lisa had no way of coping with her pregnancy. The last thing she wanted to do was get married. But after their initial revulsion to Jack, her parents joined him in an alliance to drag her to the altar.

"I'd rather have an abortion or have the baby and put it

up for adoption. I just don't want to get married," she stated clearly and firmly.

Lisa's mother, who had been divorced and remarried, was less excited about her daughter's counseling career than she was willing to admit. "Lisa, you've played the field long enough. I think it's time for you to settle down and grow up. You can't be the belle of the ball forever."

"But, Mother, I don't love him. He was fun to date but I don't want to live the rest of my life with him. He's not good enough to play college ball, and the only other thing he's done is pump gas. I don't want to marry a gas station attendant. Right now I don't want to marry anyone." Lisa was close to tears.

"Young lady, you've made your bed and now you've got to sleep in it."

"Why can't I get an abortion?"

"We can't afford it."

"Maybe Daddy would help."

"Your father hasn't sent child support in three years. Don't count on him for anything."

"What about my college plans?" Lisa was crying now.

Her mother paused, took a deep breath. "I'm not sure we could have sent you anyway. Everything's gone up so much. Besides, Jack is a fine boy. We'll all have fun planning your wedding."

"What if I refuse to marry Jack?"

"Lisa, you can't do that! The baby wouldn't have a name and we'd all be disgraced. Think about your family. You owe it to yourself and to us, to do what is right."

Lisa, who felt herself being drawn into a lifelong commitment that she didn't want, knew of no way to resist the mounting social pressure. At times she felt guilty about all the fuss she was making. Most of the girls in the class would have been happy to marry Jack. He was tall, athletic, and sexy and probably would make a good father for the baby. Maybe Mother was right. She couldn't have the world on a string forever. And her dream about being a counselor—well, dreams don't always come true.

Three days later Lisa and her mother were planning the wedding. It would be a simple affair in the pastor's study at the Nazarene Church the next Friday afternoon. Graduation was only three weeks off, but Lisa's mother didn't want her pregnancy to show when she got married, so they talked Reverend Book into doing the ceremony right away.

"My, you're going to be a busy girl these next few weeks," her aunt said to her on the phone. Lisa said yes without explaining to Aunt Jamie just how busy she would be. Part of her depression was that she couldn't honestly talk to anyone except her mother and Mother had her in a bind. Jack was the last person she wanted to talk to. He was interested in other things more than talking. He wanted to get to know her body. And all the while she screamed deep inside herself for someone to stop the whole thing.

No one was listening, so Friday at three o'clock Lisa promised to forsake all others and cling only to Jack as long as they both should live. Everyone said it was a beautiful ceremony and wished the bride and groom a million years of happy married life.

The next Monday morning everyone at school was nice to Lisa and all extended their congratulations, but a dream was dead and the whole school grieved a little. No one expressed the grief, so everybody went around with a lot of bottled-up feelings. You were supposed to say pretty things when people got married. But the hallways didn't seem very pretty that Monday, and Lisa couldn't bring herself to go to group therapy that afternoon. She had lost her kingdom and would never regain it. She was now a married woman.

Comments

An institution is a survival system of society, so we assume that it must always be good. I disagree. Institutions can change over a period of time and in such a way that they no longer serve to meet human needs. When Jesus saw that the institution of the Sabbath had ceased to have survival significance, he set out to change the institution. His first step was to show through his parables some of the inconsistencies of the institution. I have a similar purpose in relating the case stories in this chapter. I am also aware that one treads on thin ice when one defrocks a sacred cow.

Idols can be very demanding; for example, the total commitment demanded by the institution of marriage on middle-class pregnant women. The idol would accept nothing less than the total career possibility of Lisa. She now has a license to have socially approved sex and to bear offspring "with a name," but she paid an enormous price—her personhood.

Questions

Are the benefits of an unwanted marriage worth giving up a promising career?

Lisa is urged by her mother "to do what is right," get married. Why does her mother think this is "right"? Right for whom?

What other options might have been possible?

How would you respond to the option of abortion?

How would you advise your daughter with a similar problem?

The Big Wedding

St. Elizabeth's Chapel was famous for its weddings. People from all over southern Texas would reserve it months in advance. It would seat fewer than two hundred people, but it was large enough for the average wedding. The chapel had a rustic, bare wood atmosphere but not so much so that prospective brides would feel it masculine in milieu. Quite the contrary, there was a feminine fantasy about the sanctuary. The pews were white, the carpet was red, and there was a light-beige floral pattern in the draperies. The same floral motif was predominant throughout the altar area. The decor whispered, "This is a place where virgins and princes make tender promises and live happily ever after."

Dawn White fell in love with the chapel the moment she saw it. "Here comes the bride," she hummed to herself as she slid down the center aisle, her tall brunet beauty visually echoing a bride's magazine.

"I love it. I love it. I love it." There was a little girl's delight in her voice.

"It'll do," her fiancé droned.

"John, how can you say that? It's just perfect." John was as excited as Dawn about their approaching marriage, but he responded to the pomp and ceremony of a big wedding with the enthusiasm of a Texas Ranger. He would have been satisfied to exchange vows sitting on his Kawasaki motorcycle.

"I know, John, but there's something in me that needs a big church wedding."

"Have any idea what that is?"

"Well, it's all so pretty. You waiting for me at the altar with all the bridesmaids and groomsmen, and the organ announcing my entrance. And I think it will help to give our marriage a good start. How else could you begin a lifelong love relationship?"

John wasn't sure, but it was spring, the sap was rising in the trees. Dawn had refused to have sex until after the wedding. Neither of them was a virgin, but Dawn had this thing about purity and the white wedding dress.

"It just wouldn't be right to have sex and then put on that long white dress." In many ways they did have sex, but Dawn insisted that coitus, the "ultimate sex" she called it, be saved for their wedding night.

"I would like to have known you before you became a Christian."

"Don't you ever think of anything else?"

"Not often."

"I can believe it."

In the weeks prior to the wedding, Dawn became increasingly absorbed in the minutiae of the marriage planning. There was an endless checklist of activities, some dictated by etiquette and some by economics. Their initial price range was $1,500 but their cost overrun pushed them up to almost $2,000. "That's expensive sex," John's best man told him.

"Yeah, but she's worth it."

"How do you know?"

"She better be after all the hassle of this wedding." John suggested on two different occasions that they drive over to the next county and get a justice of the peace to tie the knot. Dawn would not even discuss the notion. She focused her total emotional involvement upon that twenty minutes of magic when she and John would become man and wife at St. Elizabeth's. As the big day approached, she became increasingly tense and nervous. The last-minute details were endless. Monday it was see the minister, visit the florist, check with the photographer. Tuesday it was final fitting, selection of gifts for attendants, contact the organist, call to see if number three bridesmaid was over the flu. Wednesday it was last-minute plans for the reception, selection of wines, tablecloths, and floral arrangements. Thursday was rehearsal and Friday was the great apocalyptic event. She was sure that the universe would stand still for that twenty minutes of magic and mystery.

When Dawn awoke Friday morning it was raining—hard. "Oh, no, all our dresses and flowers will be drenched." She had planned every small detail to assure that the day would be perfect. Nothing was forgotten, except the weather. By ten o'clock the skies were disgorging a liquid torrent of anger. It was the worst thunderstorm of the year. By one o'clock it was all over and the flowers were not to arrive until two. Dawn was ecstatic. The sun was shining. God himself was directing the symphonic setting of her wedding.

When the ceremony began, Dawn was nervous, but halfway down the aisle her bouquet began to shake less. When they reached the exchange of rings part of the ceremony, she was almost relaxed. She enjoyed the kiss after the declaration of spousehood and ran joyously with John up the aisle during the recessional. The reception was like Disneyland, except that it was more romantic. She was born to be a bride, some people told her, and others commented on how fantastically beautiful she was. It was a fairyland existence. Dawn hated to leave.

She began to get tense a half hour before they reached the hotel. Dawn White had had sex only twice in her life. She had been engaged before she met John and had reluctantly let her fiancé make love to her. She had performed poorly and had felt that her lack of responsiveness was a factor in the breakup of her engagement. She worried about having a problem but she was sure that sex would be different after her wedding. The wedding would wash away her guilt and make her life beautiful with John. They would drift into a passionate never-never land where the Hallelujah Chorus would accompany her climax. Abstinence before the wedding would guarantee sexual bliss after the wedding, she thought. But as they approached the hotel she was not so sure. The last time, there was pain. It hurt a lot. Her mental processes were saying that this time it would be different, but her body refused to believe her mind.

"John, I'm terribly tired." She looked directly into his eyes and begged for a sexless truce. "Let me take a nap till time for dinner."

John was speechless. Dawn had spun around so quickly upon entering the room that he passively agreed. Dawn took three tranquilizers and lay down.

After dinner John had his mind on one thing. He had waited a long time and would be put off no longer. When they reached the room, he kissed Dawn fiercely and deeply and fumbled at removing her clothes. This time, please God, he was going all the way. John had read all the books and knew the importance of foreplay. After twenty minutes of caressing every inch of her body, he expected her to be ready.

"John, please." There was panic in her voice.

"Dammit. I've waited long enough," he said to himself.

Dawn screamed! Her head was thrust back and her eyes were bulging in a death trance.

"Dammit, Dawn. I haven't done anything yet."

"Please, John." She started crying.

"What is it?"

"A terrible pain. Please wait till I can see a doctor tomorrow."

John did not perceive of himself as a total beast, so he agreed to wait. He had waited so long that one more night would not kill him. The next day they found a doctor although it wasn't easy on the weekend. The doctor told them that Dawn's hymen had already been broken and that there was no physical reason not to have coitus. He pointed out that the tenseness of a big wedding could cause muscle spasms. He gave her some exercises and sent them home. That night they did exactly what the doctor advised, but with no greater success. They were too embarrassed to go back to the doctor and tell him that his suggestions didn't work.

After a week of no success, John was furious. He insisted on a trip to a gynecologist. "What we need is a specialist." The gynecologist made a more thorough examination and prescribed the same pattern of exercises that the first doctor did. John and Dawn looked at each other but neither had the courage to tell the doctor that they had already tried his advice. That night they tried again. Still no penetration. They both were isolated in their anguish. They were exhausted by holding up the facade of a mythical good sex life. But they were too embarrassed to tell any of their family or friends the truth.

Six months after the wedding their marriage was still unconsummated, and John was talking about a divorce. One Tuesday afternoon when Dawn was driving by St. Elizabeth's she stopped and went in. Like a curious kitten in a strange place, she looked around inside the narthex. She peeped inside the bride's room where she had put on her dress, but when she came to the sanctuary she was overcome with grief. She sat down on the back pew and cried. The

94

janitor came up and asked if she was O.K. and she nodded her head yes. Then she pushed her head deep into her hands and suffered a bitter cosmic loneliness.

Comments

Unconsummated marriages are much more common than is generally known. Embarrassment prevents the spouses from telling anyone other than a physician about their problem. Physicians seldom schedule a follow-up appointment, and when the couple doesn't return they falsely assume that the problem is cured. Unknown personal pain is endured in these cases.

The bride hopes for a magical transformation at the altar but the wedding ceremony contains no mystic formula that will erase years of repressed fears and deeply embedded taboos. A big wedding can make a young woman tired, depressed, and tense. None of these feelings is conducive to the launching of a new relationship.

Questions

How could weddings be planned to avoid strain upon the bride and groom and contribute to the launching of a healthy relationship?

What needs do big weddings fulfill and for whom?

What place should the possibility of an unconsummated marriage have in marriage counseling and planning?

How can the beauty and wonder of marriage be preserved without overromanticizing?

How can the church minister to young people who are suffering the trauma of an unconsummated marriage?

The Disputed Kitchen

Becky Simpson was nineteen going on twelve. Her mother-in-law was forty-five going on eternity. Becky was a hesitant beauty, the younger sister of sisters, and bright—but not smart. For fifteen months she had fought the battle of the kitchen. There had been a hundred skirmishes and she had lost them all. Momma Simpson had the power and she held on tight. Mrs. Simpson was sweet and motherly and totally in control. She controlled every facet of her life except one —Delbert. Delbert was her only child and had been a momma's boy until he married Becky. His marriage was more an emancipation from his mother than it was a union with Becky. Since Delbert and Becky were broke, Delbert's folks had a lot to offer—money. Becky had reluctantly agreed to let them move into their apartment; there was no other way they could meet their bills.

Momma Simpson needed a child to control. When Delbert broke away, she seized his wife. Becky threatened to throw her out at least once a week, but each time she remembered those insecure feelings when she couldn't pay their bills. Collection agencies had a way of getting to Becky. She cringed every time she saw a truck drive up. "They're coming to get the furniture," she said to herself.

Papa Simpson was a noncombatant in this war. He retreated to a rocking chair and *Time* magazine. His was a rear-action battle. Mrs. Simpson had so totally seized control of him that he no longer offered a challenge. She was content to let him sit there and vegetate.

"Momma, let me dry the dishes tonight," Becky entreated the holy mother.

"Dear, you keep on asking when you know that I won't allow it."

"Well, just for tonight."

"Honey, you've been busy with the baby. This is the least that I can do," Momma Simpson said as she turned her back three-quarters on Becky.

"Where did Delbert say he was going?" the old woman wanted to know.

Becky stared at the floor. She was miserably unhappy and she knew it. Delbert was never home and Momma Simpson was never gone. Becky wanted to grab the dish towel and strangle the old woman but she had been carefully taught to respect her elders. "Don't argue with your mother" was chisled in bas-relief upon the inner walls of her brain.

"Momma, he didn't tell me."

"Listen, child, you ought to know where your husband is. Papa Simpson tried to gallivant around on me the first year we were married. I just had to let him know that I wouldn't stand for it. You've got to put your foot down with these men."

Becky stared at the linoleum. Momma Simpson knew where her weak spots were. Becky felt helpless and the helplessness soon turned into hopelessness. She was no match for her mother-in-law. She wanted to be the lady of her own house, run the kitchen the way she had learned from her own mother, establish some communication with Delbert, but all of this seemed impossible. Momma Simpson would not leave

97

unless she was rudely asked to leave. If this happened, it was back to the bill collectors.

Although Delbert made enough for them to meet their needs, his wants exceeded his income. Delbert had always gotten what he wanted. Momma Simpson saw to it that he did. So when Delbert saw the motorcycle he wanted, Momma gave him the down payment and Becky was left with the bills.

"Momma Simpson, all I want is just to dry the dishes. After all it is my kitchen." Becky shuddered as the sentence came out. It was like confronting Gabriel and the archangels.

"Becky, Becky, I know it's your kitchen. I just want to be of help. I've always taken care of Delbert and now I want to take care of you. Delbert was such a sweet boy. Never gave me a minute's trouble. Don't know what's got into him lately. I really think you ought to worry more about Delbert and let me worry about the kitchen."

Becky paused, sighed, and Momma Simpson was off on marriage lecture number twelve. She would both wash and dry the dishes while Becky stood attentive to her diatribes on how to handle a husband.

After fifteen months of kitchen torture, Becky told Delbert that he had to choose between her and his mother. With surprising ease Delbert evicted his parents, but with equal ease he left for the bar and stayed out all night.

Becky had the kitchen to herself and for the first week she enjoyed putting every item in the place she wanted it to be. The house was terribly quiet without Momma Simpson. The baby went to bed by seven and slept all night. Delbert left as soon as he changed clothes from work and was gone until two in the morning. Two weeks after the Simpsons left, Becky's only adult companionship was bill collectors.

She went to see her minister. Reverend Scott told her that she ought to make a budget and stick to it. "It'll take a lot of discipline, but it'll save your marriage. Write down on one sheet of paper Delbert's take-home pay. On another write down all of your monthly expenses. Add them up and when it comes out more than you make, then you and Delbert go back and cut out those things that you really don't need."

Becky relayed the preacher's advice to Delbert that night. His total response was one syllable, a contemptuous "Ha!" as he walked out the door. It was then that Becky's depression deepened to a danger point. She was unable to vent her anger at Delbert; she felt hopeless and alone. Her parents were seven hundred miles away.

A neighbor told her about Mary Kay cosmetics. Becky went to a demonstration and was amazed at how much better she looked. It had been so long since she had pampered herself that she found the experience intoxicating, but what was most refreshing was the acceptance of the group. Everyone seemed to think that it was O.K. for Becky to be beautiful, especially the lady who was giving the demonstration. Becky was not only sold on the product, she was fascinated by the company. She enrolled in a sales course that focused on both inner and outer beauty. The battle of the kitchen ended the day Becky gave her first demonstration. She sold seventy-five dollars' worth of merchandise and was elated. She not only knew how to look beautiful, she knew how to sell!

None of this did Becky's marriage any good. She immediately surrendered the kitchen to Momma Simpson and she threw in Delbert for good measure. She no longer felt that Delbert or the kitchen was worth fighting for. She had found herself in the most unlikely place, the selling of cosmetics.

Comments

Parents who possess their children are intolerable as in-laws. It is well known in marriage and family counseling circles that children of dysfunctional families must exert a herculean effort to escape the psychotic possessiveness of their parents. The worship of a child is as idolatrous as the worship of a spouse. And this idolatrous relationship, as all others, creates deep personal pain. The pain appears in many interpersonal areas but most vividly in the relationship between in-laws.

One of the basic structural weaknesses of the American family is its diminutive size, but numbers alone will not correct the problem. Becky had four adults living in her dwelling and was miserable. Although more than two adults is desirable, the multiplication of immaturity is a formula for pain.

Questions

How can parents learn to wean their children and still maintain a meaningful relationship with them?

At what age should such emotional weaning begin?

How can the newly married profit from the experience of their in-laws without surrendering their autonomy?

In what ways can parents relate to their sons and daughters-in-law without meddling in their lives?

How would you assess your own relationships with in-laws?

The Banker's Boy

In 1949 in Stafford Springs, Connecticut, few people had any awareness that a sexual revolution was taking place. They knew that the young people bought enough prophylactics to make it profitable to sell them in a coin-operated machine in the men's room of the Gulf station at the corner of Main and Lafayette, but few people worried about latrine merchandise. One afternoon in the fall of that year the conversation was light and frivolous in Pete's Barbershop. Frank Nicholson walked in. Frank entered with a certain confidence and bearing that only the town basketball hero could get away with. He was a unique young man and a remarkably authentic human being. Most superjocks in Stafford Springs High School were self-centered to the point of internal nausea. This was not true of Frank Nicholson. He was the most selfless man on the team. It was not unusual for him to have more assists in a game than points and his ability was such that he could score at will. At 5' 11" he was forced to play guard, but his artistry on a basketball court gave him mastery of both forecourt and backcourt. He could control the ball until some teammate was open and that teammate would get the shot.

One of the unique things about barbershops in the 1940's

was that all men were equal when that white sheet went around their necks. Barbershops were encounter groups that kept their clientele for years.

"Hey, Frank, hear you got the clap," a farmer said.

"You can hear anything in this town, Jake," Frank retorted.

"Had to get some shots, huh, Frank?"

"A couple."

"A couple, my eye. You been seeing Doc Spencer every week for a month."

"If you say so, Jake."

"Tell me, was it worth it?"

"You ought to know, Jake," and the whole barbershop laughed.

Frank was as fearless in the barber chair as he was on the basketball court. The young man had few fears, but his father was one of them. Jackson Obadiah Nicholson had been president of the Stafford Springs Savings Bank as long as anyone could remember. He was tall, gray, and warmly distinguished. Except for the pastor of the Congregational Church, there was no one in town who held more respect or power. Mr. Nicholson was the marketplace incarnate of that New England town. He symbolized as much or more than Reverend Fisher did. And he never missed a basketball game. He was cold-natured, so he sat within a few seats of the potbellied stove that heated the front of the gymnasium. At half time he would switch to the opposite side of the stove so that he could warm his other foot. Jackson Obadiah Nicholson was as out of place at a basketball game as a cat in a dog pound, but he loved Frank intensely and wanted to share this part of his life. He desperately wanted to get closer to his boy before he went off to college, and this motivated much of the old man's behavior.

So the senior Nicholson was severely shaken when he

learned that Frank had VD. He had never been able to talk to the boy, especially about matters of importance. He would have preferred to question his teller about embezzlement than to talk to Frank about VD. But he felt that he must, so he did.

"I don't know how to say this, Son, but I've heard that you've been going to the doctor to get some shots."

"I might as well tell you, Dad, I've caught syphilis but I've only got one more trip to the doctor and I'll be through."

"Through with the doctor or through with the girl?" The old man pressed his advantage.

"I don't know what you mean."

"Who did you catch it from?"

Frank looked directly at his father with an innocent savage gaze that only teen-agers can carry off. "Dad, you don't have to worry about that. I slept with a prostitute in Hartford. I'll never see her again. And I haven't had sex with any girl in town since that night, so you don't have to worry about me spreading it."

The elder Nicholson was visibly relieved and somewhat proud of the way Frank had taken care of the problem, but he found himself unable to compliment the boy lest it be taken as an endorsement of his promiscuity. "This means that you're through with girls then," the father hoped.

"Hell, no, it just means that I'm through with prostitutes."

"What's to keep you from catching it again?"

"Well, nothing, but there's a lot less chance with the girls in Stafford Springs than with the whores in Hartford." Frank was angry now. Both father and son became defensive.

"Frank, you've got a good reputation in this town and I would hate to see it ruined."

"My friends accept me and they all know that I make out with Mary Joe."

"Listen, young man, if you want to become known as the

103

town stud, you just keep on seeing Mary Joe."

"Daddy, I just don't see what is wrong with it." Frank was glad to have the whole taboo subject out in the open. "I always use contraceptives, so there's no way they can get pregnant."

"You'll lose your reputation in this town. That's what's wrong with it. A single man cannot have sex and respect both in this town. If you want to have sex, you'll have to get married."

"You know that I can't go to college if I get married."

"That's why I want you to stop."

Frank felt cornered, so he changed the focus of the conversation. "Do you believe that God created people the way they are? I mean with the human needs and the biological drives that they have?"

"Sure, what's your point?"

"Well, if God made me with a sex drive, why is it wrong for me to meet my needs if I don't hurt anyone else in the process?"

"God has nothing to do with it. The hard, cold reality of it is, that in Stafford Springs if you want to have sex and be respectable, you must be married. That's just the way it is."

"Only married people have the franchise."

"That's the way it is."

"Well, I don't accept that. It's not fair to guys like me who have to delay their marriage till they finish college. If I lose respect, it won't hurt anybody but me."

Frank's father slowly shook his head. He was losing control of the interaction and he knew it. Although he desperately wanted to remain close to Frank, something inside him pushed Frank away. "Frank, do you know what I overheard at the hardware store yesterday? I was two counters over and they didn't see me. They were talking about you going to see

Doctor Spencer and one of the ladies said, 'And he's the banker's boy.' "

"Who cares what old ladies say?"

"I care. The bank depends upon my reputation."

"Daddy, I don't believe anything me and Mary Joe do is going to hurt your bank."

"That's where you're wrong." Nicholson wished he had not said it, but once it was out he lacked the courage to take it back. Frank knew the conversation was over, so he sat mutely. His father was unable to change either his boy's behavior or the mores of Stafford Springs. The last thing he wanted to happen was to find himself defending the town against Frank. Although the old man, feeling the impasse between himself and his son growing, was sad to see it happen, he could not express his sadness. If he could have shouted, "Frank I don't want to see us growing apart because of this," much of the impasse would have parted, but he couldn't say it. The two sat silently for a long while. It was the last time they would ever discuss anything of survival significance. Frank was not only forced to choose between sex and the mores of the town, he was also forced to choose between his father and himself.

"Good-by, Daddy, I'm going to basketball practice," he said as he climbed on his bike and kicked up the stand. Basketball and football were supposed to exhaust young men to the point that they wouldn't have enough energy to crawl in the backseat and do anything more than kiss. But times were changing, and Frank was very much a part of his time. The following Friday night he got the car and he and Mary Joe parked behind the Baptist Church on the south side of town.

Comments

The franchise of sex is exclusively owned by the institution of marriage, but the franchise is not secure. It is thought that institutions are internally tough and capable of sustaining endless attack. Not so! Institutions are most delicate and are extremely sensitive to forces that threaten them. The liberalizing of sex mores is a major threat to the institution of marriage. The tide of free love has not been held back, but the institution has fought it every inch of the way.

Do the unmarried and the divorced (those outside the institution) merit the opportunity to meet their emotional and sexual needs? To what extent has our culture declared the unmarried and the divorced as nonpersons? Economically? Socially? Spiritually? Sexually? Does the church have an obligation to minister to the adult unmarrieds? If so, how?

Questions

Since sexuality is a good gift of God, why restrict its expression by unconditional vows of fidelity to one person?

How can the emotional and sexual needs of unmarried and divorced persons be met?

If you were Frank's father, how would you have tried to reason with him?

In what ways does your church attempt to minister to single and divorced persons?

Where do we seek ethical guidelines in an age of moral transition?

The Unpardonable Sin

Edith looked and acted more like the wife of a minister than she did the wife of a buyer for Sears, Roebuck. She was attractive in a reserved kind of way. She used makeup sparingly but her paleness was neither chic nor natural, it was simply drab. Although she had all the raw material of a beautiful appearance, there was some hesitancy on her part about letting the end product come out looking beautiful. Her mother had once criticized her for admiring herself in the mirror. "Who would stop a galloping horse to look at you?" Mother had said. The word "vanity" had been buried deeply in her bones, just where Mother wanted it. Edith had enough natural beauty to stop a cavalry charge if she had really looked her best. Afterward she would have felt guilty about it. "You aren't supposed to enjoy yourself," played over and over in her head. Edith, according to her husband, was a poor housekeeper, but here ended her list of liabilities. A good mother, a devoted wife, a loyal companion, and an ideal spouse, she was ready to move wherever Sears wanted Jason. For all of this, Jason loved her dearly.

Jason was a missionary masquerading as a buyer for Sears. His principal words were "should," "ought," "have to," "must." He lived his life in the imperative mode and, like

Edith, he was as hard on himself as he was on others. Jason had many good qualities that he failed to enjoy because he was constantly telling himself that he ought to be a better man than he was. He was patient and tender and playful with the children. He also expected perfection in his parenthood, and when this didn't happen he put himself down for being a bad parent.

It was this same kind of "ought" that almost ended his marriage. He felt as though he ought to tell Edith everything that happened. To say that traveling businessmen are promiscuous would be a generalization, but perhaps not a bad one. When for weeks at a time a man is away from home and family, the local girls look better each passing day. Jason was different. He traveled the wholesale buying circuit for five years and never touched a woman. At times he wanted to so badly that his bones ached, but his internal ought machine was in good working condition and he toughed it out. One night in Dallas he went downtown with his partner and had a few drinks. They both wound up in bed with a pair of Texas beauties. When Jason sobered up, his ought machine punished him, all the way back to New Orleans. He worried for a week about having caught VD. When this failed to develop he felt obligated to go to confession. The priest was named Edith.

"Jason, how could you do this to me? After all of these years, how could you be unfaithful to me and the children?" Halfway through the last word her lower lip quivered, her voice broke, and the waterworks began. Jason tried to put his arm around her but she was untouchable.

Edith knew that her pastor was not in the divorce business and she felt sure he would be supportive in her grief. This was what she wanted. The day after Jason had confessed his "one-night stand" she had decided to get a divorce. But she wanted to discuss her plans with Reverend Robertson before she went to the expense of hiring an attorney. Edith's first surprise was that her pastor did not flinch with shock when she told him about Jason. He heard her story but he didn't use the word "awful" or "terrible" or "disgusting."

"Edith, I can tell that you are bothered by all of this, but I'm at a loss as to what you want me to do." At this point Edith was more confused than ever. Where was the reverend's righteous indignation? Perhaps he thought that she had been promiscuous too.

"Mr. Robertson, Jason is the only man I've ever had sex with. We agreed that this was sacred and that we would not share it with anyone else. But Jason has broken his marriage vows, and I'm going to get a divorce." Perhaps he would understand now and realize how awful a thing Jason had done.

"Are there other reasons?"

"No, and that's what's so terrible. Except for this, Jason has been a wonderful husband. Why did he have to go and ruin a beautiful marriage?"

"Do you still love him?"

Edith didn't expect the question. She had cognitively decided that their relationship was over and that her love for Jason was dead, but she found herself unable to say that she didn't love him. "I suppose I do. But I can't keep on loving him after what he's done, can I?"

"Edith, a part of my religious convictions is a thing called forgiveness. It's also a part of my wife's faith, and if it weren't, we wouldn't be married today."

"I know, but I just can't trust Jason anymore. If he did it once, he'll do it again."

"What makes you so sure about that?"

"Well, this just shows that there is something wrong deep down inside Jason. If there wasn't, he would never have done it."

Mr. Robertson had difficulty playing counselor at this point. At times his parishioners simply needed to be enlightened. He put on his teacher's hat and said to Edith: "I find it hard to believe that human beings are monogamous by nature. I can remember watching the geese on our farm back in Arkansas. They would mate only once, and if a gander's mate died, he would never mate again. But I don't believe people are this way. People can be trained and conditioned to be monogamous but they don't come by it naturally. So I don't think Jason's one night with another woman indicates that there is anything basically wrong with him. His conditioning just broke down for one night."

"But there's still this deep, dark stain on him that won't wash off."

"You mean like he's committed the unpardonable sin?"

"Yes, that's right."

Robertson put on his teaching hat again. "I find that the idea of the unpardonable sin is a creation of man and not of God. People at times find it difficult to forgive certain behavior because they feel threatened by it. But the God described in the Bible is always open and ready for reconciliation with his children."

"Now, you're putting the burden of saving the marriage on me," Edith protested. "It was Jason who caused this whole thing."

"From what you tell me, Jason wants very much to keep the marriage, is that right?"

Edith nodded and looked at the floor.

"So if the relationship is saved, it depends on your willingness to see his behavior as a one-time thing and not as a symptom of some basic character fault." Robertson was moving faster than Edith could follow, and he sensed this. He backed up and said, "Edith, you may feel that Jason's affair was the beginning of the end of your relationship and that

110

you wanted to spare yourself the pain of a long marriage illness, if the thing was going to die anyway."

"Yes, that's right. I felt that a cancer had come into our marriage and that I didn't want the thing to drag on. There would be less pain if we just broke it off quickly."

"I can see," Robertson added, "that the only problem is that you're married to a man and not a goose. Your diagnosis might have been accurate for a gander, but it wasn't accurate for Jason."

"Men are promiscuous by nature?" she asked in unbelief.

"Women too!" he answered without blinking.

"I've never wanted to have sex with anyone other than Jason."

"I don't believe you," Robertson countered. If the confrontation had come from anyone else, Edith would have felt like she was being called a loose woman, but there was acceptance as well as confrontation in Robertson's tone.

"Well, maybe before we were married when I was in high school, but not since Jason and I got married." Her tone heightened as she ended the sentence.

"I still don't believe you." His encounter was almost sensuous.

"You mean that you think that I still want to have sex with other men?"

"That's right."

"What makes you think that?"

"Because you're a woman and not a goose."

Edith laughed and felt better. "My mother would roll over in her grave if she knew her daughter was being taught things like this in church."

"I expect she would." Robertson laughed. "Are you ready for some problem solving?" he inquired after a moment.

"Yeah, what do I do about Jason?" Edith wanted to know.

"Would you like for him to do penance?"

"Yeah, he ought not to get off scot-free."

"Call him and have him meet you at the most expensive restaurant in town. And if you want to have a cry and a little chat before you go in, you can do that in the car."

"My mother would consider you a dirty old man, Mr. Robertson."

"She might be right about that." They both laughed.

"Could I use your phone to call Jason?"

"Sure."

Edith got up and walked around the chair to the desk. As she did, Mr. Robertson noticed her shapely curves and he laughed to himself about his own promiscuity.

Comments

The promiscuous tendencies of the human animal are not romantic to think about; the church has refused to think about them and the marketplace has worked hard to keep them in the dark shadows of taboo. Jesus dealt frankly with the subject on the occasion of "the woman caught in the act of adultery" (John 8:3).

Questions

Why did Edith find one act of sexual infidelity to be virtually unforgivable?

How would you feel if the same thing happened to you?

How do we learn to be forgiving?

Why is sexuality so difficult to discuss openly, particularly in the church?

If we really accepted our sexuality as a good gift of God, how would our attitudes change?

112

The Trapped Couple

She slammed the door and didn't look back. Defiantly she strode to the car. Tires squealed as Ruth spun out of the driveway and blasted down the street. Art had never seen her drive like this. He waited. "She'll be back in half an hour," he reassured himself. An hour later he began to worry. Three hours later when she had not returned, he called the police. He checked to see if the car had been in an accident. No word and no Ruth. "I really blew it this time," he said out loud.

Ruth and Art had been married seven years and the past year everything had gone wrong. They had quarreled over the kids. They had difficulty discussing any matter of importance. There was a wall between them and it was growing thicker. Art had always been the dominant member of the family and he felt that it ought to be this way. But in the last year, Ruth had wanted more say in family decisions. Art blamed women's lib for messing with her mind. Ruth denied it. She kept saying that she had as much right to be on this planet as anyone. "You're acting like you own it," Art would answer, and a fight was on. The past two weeks had been war and the peace treaty had not yet been signed.

Ruth was in her mid-thirties and more beautiful than the day Art married her. She had a dark Latin loveliness. Her

113

mother, who was Mexican American, was more submissive than she. "You should have married my mother," Ruth shouted in a moment of anger. Art knew that his wife was twice the woman that her mother was. Ruth could express her feelings both good and bad. She was sensitive and understanding, and with the children she was both patient and firm. There was no way Art wanted to lose her, but her recent assertiveness was driving him up the wall. Art, the oldest of two brothers and one sister, had always been boss, especially with his little sister. He thought he had married Ruth for her good looks, but he now realized that he was more attracted to her submissiveness.

Both Ruth and Art had come from big families. Art's grandparents lived at his house. His grandfather owned half the farm and raised cattle. There were at least four adults and four kids in the house during most of his childhood. And for some reason that he couldn't express, Art felt something was missing in his suburban home with Ruth and the girls. Ruth's uncle had lived at her house for as long as she could remember and her grandparents lived next door. She fondly remembered her upbringing. Art had spent his happiest days branding calves with his grandfather. The table talk at his childhood home was an exciting review of cattle, farming, and people. In some ways it was like an encounter group but it had a genuineness and reality that no therapy group ever achieved.

Ruth remembered a typical afternoon at Grandma's house. She would run up the sidewalk to the front porch and her grandmother would say: "Ruth, Ruth, I've been thinking about you all day long. I'm so glad to see you." And the old woman would put her arms around her and, after a warm, tight hug, the two of them would sit and talk.

Art called the police again. Still no word on his wife or his station wagon. He checked with Ruth's friends. He just hoped to God she hadn't taken off for New Mexico, but that was a two-day drive and he didn't think she would leave without the kids. Art fantasized the cataclysmic tragedies that pollute people's minds when they are going through a private storm. How would he go about telling the girls that their mother had been killed in a car wreck because he had driven her out of the house? Or worse still, maybe she did go to New Mexico and had decided not to come back.

It was two o'clock in the morning when the station wagon drove up. Art was both relieved and angry but the anger melted into reconciliation when he saw how hard Ruth was crying. They embraced each other for a long time. When Ruth stopped crying she said: "It's just not right, the way we're living. Honey, both of us were brought up in big families. I've been blaming you for my misery when it's not your fault at all. I've fought you about everything because the fighting took my mind off the real problem."

"What's that?" Art hesitantly asked.

"Honey, we're isolated. It's just you and me and the girls. We've got friends but friends don't make a family."

"What do you want to do?"

"I don't know." Ruth was crying again.

"We could sell the house and go back to Santa Fe." Art sounded uncertain as he said it.

"But what about your job? You couldn't just quit your job. All your schooling and everything." Ruth had been excited when they first moved to Kansas City. Art had done well in his company and the move meant a promotion. At $25,000 a year they were living well and only two years ago had bought a new house. The first year the house alone had kept them busy, but when the new wore off and the yard was in, their problems began.

"I couldn't earn this kind of money in Santa Fe but we could live on less than we're making. There's nothing about

115

this rat race that I really like except the money."

Ruth began to drift in her thinking as people do when they are struggling between what is and what ought to be. "While I was out driving, I cried and cried and eventually I stopped feeling sorry for myself. And all of a sudden it struck me. I had been blaming you for all of our problems. Maybe neither of us is to blame. Maybe the suburban way we're living is all wrong. I don't mean just wrong for us. I mean wrong for everybody. Our whole community is divorced. We're all divorced from each other. The only difference between us and divorced persons is that they've got more courage. They hurt as much or more than we do but at least they have the guts to do something."

"You're right," Art said. "I can raise hogs back on the farm and give you a better life than this. The girls have forgotten what a grandmother is. And if you mention aunts or uncles, you have to stop and define the word."

"Maybe we're just homesick and need a vacation." Ruth wavered for a moment. She was both hopeful and fearful that Art might suggest that they do something.

"No, it's more than that. We need to change the way we're living. I need some male companionship. I think that I would be less bossy if I had it."

"What do you want to do?"

"I'll talk to a realtor tomorrow and call home tonight. We need to sell the house and I need a job in Santa Fe, if we're going to make a move. What do you want?"

"I'll be happy with anything that you're happy with."

That night Art called home and he received the first of the bad news. The farm could barely support his two brothers. The summer had been dry and beef prices were way down. His youngest brother promised to look around town for a job but he wasn't hopeful. It was hard to get a clerk's job in a department store. The next day Art learned that he would

116

have to take a loss if he sold the house. Since two large plants had closed, the market was flooded with low-equity homes for sale. Renting the house would be impossible. Art figured that they still owed $2,500 on the station wagon.

"Why couldn't we just walk away and leave the house? We don't have that much money in it." Ruth wanted to know.

"We'd lose our credit. Never be able to borrow again."

Ruth was pale. "We're trapped. We're in a vicious suburban trap. If we stay here, our marriage is ruined, and if we leave, our credit is ruined." She began to cry softly.

Art put his arm around her. "There are other alternatives. I'll get an appointment with a marriage counselor tomorrow. They are specialists who work with our kind of problem. A friend of mine at work said he and his wife got lots of help."

Although Ruth had some hesitation about discussing their intimate problems with a stranger, the following week they both went to counseling. For a little while things did get better, but there was no way the counselor could change the structure of the community in which she lived and this was what Ruth really wanted.

Comments

There is a lingering remembrance of the extended family. Some adults can remember when the family unit contained as many as twelve people. With a dozen people the repertoire of possible interactions was geometrically greater than it is with the three or four in today's family. Family life has become colorless and, for those adults who can remember the rainbow of the extended family, this is a bitter black and white. The current wave of nostalgia is a wistful glance at a time when some of our basic social institutions were different.

Questions

To what extent does the story of the trapped couple reflect your own life?

If you have avoided the trap, how did you do it?

What were the advantages and liabilities of the extended family of earlier times?

What are the features of contemporary living patterns that are unfulfilling?

What practical steps could you propose to change them?

5
What to Do About It

Marriage is an institution and as such it is a survival system of society, but we have made it more than that. We have made it a god, a panacea for the problems of the Western world, the foundation of our economy, a puberty rite for proving personhood, a romantic ritual for entrance into society, an exclusive franchise for socially approved sex, and a source of correction for one's own inner deficiencies. Too much! No pagan ever asked so much from any gilded idol.

Marriage is a socially accepted relationship between two persons, designed to meet their interpersonal needs. If the institution fails in the sole mission of meeting human needs, it must be restructured.

It is not my purpose to abolish the dyad, or to recommend communes, or to return to the extended family. I consider all these options untenable. They will not work for most Americans. My goal is to expand the economic involvement of the dyad in such a way that people can grow old with more dignity and less pain.

I consider the American marketplace the most productive arena in the history of mankind. I would do nothing to change its basic structure or to weaken its productivity. But the marketplace doesn't have a thermometer that measures

121

the quality of human life, nor should it have one. This is neither the role nor the purpose of the market. This qualitative, prophetic judgment is the task of the church.

The principal purpose of this book is to communicate this judgment through case stories, but there are some tangible, practical patterns of interpersonal living that are effective in correcting the dysfunctional nature of the institution of marriage.

I

It is chauvinistic to assume that only the male spouse should possess a marketable skill. Women who fail to train themselves to do something of survival value in the community are risking the most unpleasant possible experience, that of being thrown away. Most men in our culture have worked hard to avoid this traumatic possibility. Women should also. Even the widow who is financially "taken care of" will be emotionally and socially discarded if she cannot actively contribute to the well-being of the community after her husband's death.

Mothering is a full-time job of survival significance but only for a fraction of a woman's life. Life-time mothers are, in general, displaced persons in the American community. Many women complete their college or professional training in their late teens or early twenties. Then they rear children and lose their professional skills or they maintain their professional skills and neglect their children. Women who rear their children first and then obtain their vocational training can order their lives in a much more meaningful pattern. A knowledge of chemistry contributes nothing to the rearing of children but a knowledge of chemistry that is obtained after the children are reared is a valuable tool for building a career in the community. Women whose children are school age

122

should begin to retool themselves for a nonmothering career or they will be discarded by the powerful forces of the marketplace. This is neither awful nor terrible, it is simply the way it is.

II

The quality of human life is measurably improved when couples spend more time in groups. The dyad can be enriched if it is willing to be exposed to a larger repertoire of possible interactions. There are fun groups, church groups, problem-solving groups, encounter groups, all offering this possibility.

In my youth there was only one television set in town. It was located in the basement of the Presbyterian Church and the whole community would gather to watch television. It was a meaningful group experience, but the dyad doesn't watch television this way anymore. It isolates itself in monastic solitude and listens to commercials telling how wonderful it all is.

We let our affluence keep us apart. Historically, a sense of community has developed at the place where people cook their bread and wash their clothes. Even at a washateria there can be a limited group involvement but most homes in middle America have their own washing machine, their own oven, and one or more television sets, so the dyad has a tendency to center around these objects. For this reason a conscious cognitive effort must be made to get more group exposure. The marketplace itself provides a group experience but seldom does it provide the same experience for both spouses. Most Americans do not experience a group involvement of survival significance until they are admitted to a hospital and then they are too sick to enjoy it.

The encounter group movement has rediscovered what people have instinctively known for centuries. Heterogeneous groups are richer, more exciting, more meaningful than homogeneous groups. A deep intergroup experience seldom happens with fewer than six persons, and the six should be of both sexes and various age levels. There is a symphony of human interactions available for a modest investment of time and money, but the dyad that places itself under house arrest will hear only the dink, dink, dink of its own duality.

III

While the dyad needs more group exposure, individuals need more privacy. The romantic dualism of the modern marriage myth interprets a need for privacy as a lack of love, "If you want to be by yourself, then you must not love me anymore." People are conditioned to feel guilty about their need for privacy. Few people pray anymore, so the beauty of a human being in true privacy with the eternal is a lost art.

The human animal needs privacy as much as it needs intimacy and it is not prepared for the latter until it has experienced the former. Many couples do not fully enjoy each other until one member has just returned from a trip that enabled both members to experience a degree of privacy.

Business trips are as much for the salvation of marriages as they are for the well-being of the marketplace. In counseling circles, this is called structured distancing—an expensive way to get privacy, available to only a small percentage of people. But privacy is as available as a walk down the street, when you affirm your need for it by saying, "This is a normal human requirement that I am taking care of."

Unfortunately, certain marriage enrichment groups do not realize the basic need that people have for privacy. Some enrichment groups teach that personal privacy is the arch-enemy of intimacy and that the need for it must be destroyed before intimacy can be achieved. In reality people need both privacy and intimacy.

Real privacy is available through prayer and meditation, but for many people this is an option that ceased when they joined the church of romanticism. For the nonreligious, mystic meditation is the in thing. If you are athletically inclined, a five-mile run is a beautiful source of privacy that will seldom be interrupted. Only a priest saying Mass is more secure in his privacy.

IV

The best single antidote for the poison of dualism is a joint economic involvement with another couple. Two families can afford three times as much as one family can. The recreational vehicle industry offers an unlimited source of equipment that can help to structure free time in a functional manner. (Most marriage problems develop on weekends.) The problem is that the average American family cannot afford thirty thousand dollars to buy a sailboat, but two or three families can.

Since multifamily purchases are more complicated than single-family purchases, many couples are scared away. Personality clashes occur. Jealousy over utilization of the vehicle develops. People are conditioned to say "my boat," "my plane," "my camper." The more dominant individuals in the partnership may want to dictate the structure of the agreement. Power struggles result. Passive-aggressive behavior will sabotage the best-laid plans. The whole interpersonal plot thickens. Wonderful! These problems must be solved, but the honest effort of four or more adults to work through them will produce a quality of human life that far surpasses anything the dyad can achieve on its own.

Ambiguity must be avoided or the partnership will not survive. The utilization of any significant joint purchase should be clearly defined in a written partnership agreement. Family A has utilization X number of days, family B and family C have utilization an equal number of days. The common purchase will bring the families together, but exclusive separate time-frames will allow for privacy. John may want to fly the plane to North Dakota all by himself. He can do this in his own time-frame without hurt feelings.

The death of any or all of the partners must be considered, discussed, and detailed in the partnership agreement. How do you pay off the mortgage? Do surviving partners have first option to buy? Do estates assume costs and pay deficits? Is the partnership binding on heirs, executors, and administrators of the estates?

Responsibility for maintenance and repairs should be clearly delineated. Transfer of the vehicle or property from one family to another should be spelled out in writing. Overt written agreements are necessary for a family that is exploring for the first time the frontier of joint economic involvement.

V

Romanticism is a conditioned response. It is not the natural state of human beings. It is a learned life-style, and it can be unlearned. Romanticism conditions people to think that they can actualize themselves only in a romantic relationship. Most of the music that is pumped into your home, office, car, and camper is blatant romanticism. It is seldom that you can turn on your transistor radio without subjecting yourself to this conditioning process.

But the process can be reversed. The good news is this: authentic relationships are possible, people are precious, and

126

beautiful interactions are born every day. There are four steps in the process of deromanticizing yourself. First, you must become aware of the conditioning process. You must say: "Hey, what is this song trying to communicate? What is this commercial trying to say?" Second, once awareness is achieved you are in a position to make a cognitive denial. You can say, "I don't believe that." You can refuse to accept the assumptions of the myth. Third, you must expose yourself to group interactions. This may be in an encounter group or in your church or in your club. The only requirement is to find a dozen people who are open and honest and have the courage and ability to express their feelings. Fourth, you must make an economic adventure with another couple.